Using SOLO Taxonomy to Think Like a Scientist

How to develop curious minds with the science capabilities

The Material World

Use evidence

Interpret representations

Gather and interpret data

Critique evidence

Engage with science

Pam Hook and Willem Tolhoek

Title:	Using SOLO Taxonomy to Think Like a Scientist How to develop curious minds with the science capabilities – The Material World
Authors:	Pam Hook and Willem Tolhoek
Editor:	Tanya Tremewan
Designer:	Diane Williams
Book code:	51013
ISBN:	978-1-77655-392-1
Published:	2017
Publisher:	Essential Resources Educational Publishers Limited

United Kingdom:	Australia:	New Zealand:
Units 8–10 Parkside	PO Box 906	PO Box 5036
Shortgate Lane	Strawberry Hills	Invercargill
Laughton BN8 6DG	NSW 2012	
ph: 0845 3636 147	ph: 1800 005 068	ph: 0800 087 376
fax: 0845 3636 148	fax: 1800 981 213	fax: 0800 937 825

Websites:	www.essentialresourcesuk.com www.essentialresources.com.au www.essentialresources.co.nz
Copyright:	Text: © Pam Hook and Willem Tolhoek, 2017 Edition and illustrations: © Essential Resources Educational Publishers Limited, 2017
About the authors:	Pam Hook is an educational consultant (HookED www.pamhook.com), who works with New Zealand and Australian schools to develop curricula and pedagogies for learning to learn based on SOLO Taxonomy. She has published articles on thinking, learning, e-learning and gifted education, and written curriculum material for government and business. She is author and coauthor of more than 15 books on SOLO Taxonomy including titles translated into Danish, and is coauthor of two science textbooks widely used in New Zealand secondary schools. She is a popular keynote speaker at conferences. Willem Tolhoek has been a science educator in New Zealand secondary schools since 2005. He has a passion for developing literacy and engaging students in science. While in an acting HOLA Science role over the last four years, he has worked with Pam Hook to further integrate the use of SOLO in the science curriculum to develop students' surface level of thinking to a deeper level of understanding. Willem is a proud father to his daughter Isobel and is thankful for the support of his partner Tegan.
Acknowledgements:	Thanks to Professor John Biggs for his encouragement and ongoing critique of our work with the classroom-based approach to using SOLO Taxonomy and to the many teachers and schools around the world who are using SOLO Taxonomy to make surface and deep understanding visible to students. Special thanks to staff and students at Lincoln High School (Canterbury, New Zealand) for the examples used in the book.

Copyright notice:

All rights reserved. No part of this publication may be reproduced, stored in a retrieval system, or transmitted in any form by any means, electronic or mechanical or by photocopying, recording or otherwise, without the prior written permission of the publisher. Copyright owners may take legal action against a person or organisation who infringes their copyright through unauthorised copying. All inquiries should be directed to the publisher at the address above.

Contents

Introduction	**4**
1. An overview of SOLO Taxonomy and thinking like a scientist	**5**
What is SOLO Taxonomy?	5
What is thinking like a scientist?	6
What is the material world?	8
How can SOLO help develop curious minds with the science capabilities?	11
2. Gather and interpret data	**19**
Gathering data (multistructural level)	19
Interpreting data (relational level)	21
Strategies for gathering and interpreting data	23
3. Use evidence	**41**
Using evidence (relational level)	41
Strategies for using evidence	42
4. Critique evidence	**46**
Critiquing evidence (extended abstract level)	46
Reliability and validity	47
Challenging evidence that seems reliable	48
Fairness, completeness and relevance	50
Strategies for critiquing evidence	50
5. Interpret representations	**54**
Interpreting representations (extended abstract level)	54
Strategies for interpreting representations	57
6. Sample SOLO planning and assessment	**62**
Constructive alignment in planning and assessment	62
Sample planning	63
Sample assessment	65
7. Engage with science	**68**
Engaging with science (extended abstract level)	68
Bringing in ideas about a waste management issue (multistructural level)	72
Connecting ideas about a waste management issue (relational level)	73
Extending ideas about a waste management issue (extended abstract level)	74
Conclusions	**76**
References	**77**
Index of exhibits	**78**

Introduction

To think like a scientist is to be curious about the natural and physical worlds. Curiosity is central to both science and innovation. Science and innovation are central to New Zealand's economic, environmental, social and cultural wellbeing.[1] Curiosity matters most when it develops in the context of collaboration, citizenship and community.

In this book we share ways to spark this curiosity, deep learning and engagement in science using the classroom approach to SOLO Taxonomy (Biggs and Collis 1982; Hook 2016) and the science capabilities. We do this in the context of the material world strand in the New Zealand Science Curriculum (NZC).

Sections are framed against each science capability. They show how using SOLO along with current theories on how students learn and the effective pedagogies that lead to iterative, complex and deep learning helps students' curiosity when thinking with the science capabilities about the everyday science of common materials and waste management.

The timely book provides a strong model for what it takes to develop students' citizen-centric scientific curiosity in a world facing significant challenges. "Doing the right thing" today is an increasingly complex problem for all ages, requiring many diverse perspectives for what can only be fuzzy solutions. Students are never too young to think with the science capabilities – using this approach, even curious five-year-olds can discover scientific meaning that contributes something of value to the larger scientific community.

In adopting a strengths-based approach to thinking like a scientist with the different science capabilities, we can align science content with notions of citizenship and the social good. With the material world strand, students can use waste management as a context for engaging in science (see Section 7). This link demonstrates how being curious about science enables students to feel like they belong, matter, are heard and can make a difference in their world.

As well as building curiosity, sharing SOLO as a model of learning helps student build capabilities as self-regulatory learners. Students develop self-regulatory capability when they have access to "success criteria, planning and prediction, having intentions to implement goals, setting standards for self-judgements and the difficulty of goals" (Hattie and Donoghue 2016). Teachers and students themselves comment on how self-regulatory behaviours develop using SOLO strategies for deep learning in science (see quotes below and later in this book). This book includes many examples of how the criteria for self-regulatory learning are made accessible and visible when teachers share SOLO and SOLO strategies with students.

> *I like using SOLO strategies like the maps, rubrics and hexagons because they help me organise and plan out my thoughts, as well as allowing me to make links between concepts and develop them to higher levels of thinking. (Student, Lincoln High School)*

> *SOLO hexagons are really helpful as they allow me to link subtopics and key ideas together. The ability to do this is really important in science as one topic is usually related to more than one other topic. (Student, Lincoln High School)*

> *SOLO Describe++ maps and rubrics (see, think, wonder maps) let me take a basic science concept and develop it further to give me a better understanding. The "see" is the basic idea that I understand, the "think" unpacks this basic concept, and the "wonder" allows me to think beyond the concept to make links to the wider world. (Student, Lincoln High School)*

---

1   See New Zealand's national strategic plan for science in society (Ministry of Business, Innovation and Employment et al 2014).

1. An overview of SOLO Taxonomy and thinking like a scientist

This section establishes the foundations for the discussion that follows by clarifying what we mean by SOLO Taxonomy, thinking like a scientist, material world and using SOLO when developing curious minds with the science capabilities.

What is SOLO Taxonomy?

> *SOLO is a flexible framework that allows my students to self-evaluate their learning and determine their next steps.* (Science teacher, Lincoln High School)

Structure of the Observed Learning Outcome (SOLO) Taxonomy is an evidence-based model of learning that university academics Biggs and Collis developed in the late 1970s based on research exploring the structure of samples of student thinking in many different subjects (and across many different levels). It represents the increasing structural complexity of learning outcomes as learning progresses through surface, deep and conceptual levels of understanding (Biggs and Collis 1982).

SOLO has a long history of use at a tertiary level where it is used to design courses and assess course outcomes, mark academic theses and determine the effect of different research interventions. New Zealand schools began to use it as a common language of learning, along with SOLO-based learning strategies, in 2003. It is used in classrooms to plan, monitor and assess learning. It makes the complexity of the learning task and learning outcome visible to students so that they can reflect on what they are doing, how well it is going and their next steps in learning.

The model describes five distinct levels of learning outcomes that show: no idea (prestructural), one idea (unistructural), several ideas (multistructural), related ideas (relational) and extended ideas (extended abstract). Teachers share these levels with their students using names, symbols and hand signs for the levels, as well as academic verbs matched to each level (Exhibit 1.1).

Exhibit 1.1: SOLO levels shown through names, symbols, hand signs and academic verbs

Prestructural No idea	Unistructural One idea	Multistructural Many ideas	Relational Related ideas	Extended abstract Extended ideas
Learning outcomes show unconnected information, no organisation.	Learning outcomes show simple connections but importance is not noted.	Learning outcomes show connections are made, but significance to overall meaning is missing.	Learning outcomes show full connections made, and synthesis of parts to the overall meaning.	Learning outcomes go beyond subject and make links to other concepts.
	define, name, label, identify	*describe, list, elaborate*	*sequence, classify, compare, contrast, explain causes, explain effects, analyse*	*generalise, predict, evaluate, create*

As learning progresses, the SOLO levels represent two changes in the learning outcome. First, the learner increases quantitatively in understanding (bringing in ideas – knowing more, moving from unistructural to multistructural outcomes). Second, their understanding changes qualitatively (linking ideas and extending ideas – deepening understanding when moving from multistructural to relational to extended abstract outcomes) (Biggs and Tang 2007).

In the classroom, students and teachers use the model to describe the cognitive complexity of a learning outcome and how learning outcomes change and become more complex as any academic task is mastered (Biggs 1999). In this way SOLO makes visible both: the structure of learning – loose, connected or extended ideas; and the process of learning – moving from idea to ideas to related ideas to extended ideas.

The focus is on the complexity of the structure of the learning task and the student response, rather than on categorising students themselves. In this way the model focuses us on "what the student does" rather than "what the student is" or "what the teacher does" (Biggs and Tang 2007, p 16). It differentiates by both task and outcome.

Just as there are "different horses for different courses" so there are different learning strategies for different stages of the learning process. Making the cognitive complexity of the task visible with SOLO makes it easier to select effective learning strategies. These SOLO-aligned learning interventions cover bringing in ideas (multistructural), relating ideas (relational) and extending ideas and looking at them in a new way (extended abstract) (Exhibit 1.2).

Exhibit 1.2: Examples of thinking strategies and e-learning strategies differentiated against SOLO levels

Unistructural	Multistructural	Relational	Extended abstract
Strategies for bringing in ideas		Strategies for connecting ideas	Strategies for extending ideas
Make links with prior knowledge Writing in your own words Mnemonics Underlining and highlighting HOT SOLO Define map and rubric de Bono Red Hat thinking Google "Define" strategy	Rehearsal and memorisation HookED SOLO hexagons HOT SOLO Describe map and rubric de Bono White Hat thinking Brainstorming Instagrok: www.instagrok.com	HookED SOLO hexagons HOT SOLO Sequence, Classify, Compare and Contrast, Analyse maps and rubrics HookED SOLO Explain causes, Explain effects, Analogy maps and rubrics de Bono Yellow Hat and Black Hat thinking de Bono CoRT Plus Minus Interesting routine Explain Everything app: www.morriscooke.com	HookED SOLO hexagons HOT SOLO Generalise, Predict, Evaluate maps and rubrics HookED SOLO Describe++ map and rubric de Bono Blue Hat and Green Hat thinking "What if" questions Rationale: http://rationale.austhink.com Values Exchange all schools project: www.vxcommunity.com

This process allows teachers to identify cognitively appropriate learning interventions in thinking and e-learning for each student. Students can use the same process to identify where they are in the learning process, and what thinking strategies and use of technologies will help them progress, thus creating their own toolbox for learning (Hook 2012).

What is thinking like a scientist?

Aah, there's nothing more exciting than science. You get all the fun of sitting still, being quiet, writing down numbers, paying attention ... Science has it all. (Principal Skinner, *The Simpsons*)

Many teachers will tell you there is more to thinking like a scientist than Principal Skinner describes. However, there is also more to science than simply "being curious" and "doing lots of experiments". All that observing and inferring when mixing chemicals, setting materials on fire or dissecting earthworms is of little consequence without the relevant science vocabulary and knowledge to *describe* what we observe and *explain* how and why what we observe or measure connects to the natural and physical worlds. Without science language and content knowledge, hands-on science is little more than edutainment, magic tricks or "busy work". Furthermore, setting the expectation that science is all about flashy explosions, making nasty smells and dancing raisins may compromise students' enthusiasm and patience for the joys to be found in more measured and deeper study in the future.

To think (and act) like a scientist is all about noticing and interpreting things that make us curious – making and then verifying meaning. It involves skilled and active creative and critical thinking. That is, it is to be ready, willing and able to explore and make decisions about the scientific phenomena that make us curious in the natural and physical worlds – and then, importantly, to be open to changing those decisions whenever curious minds bring new evidence to light. Thinking like a scientist is to:

- know about thinking like a scientist (content – knowing about)
- know how to think like a scientist (skill – knowing how to)
- have the will to think like a scientist (disposition – will)
- act on opportunities to think like a scientist (behaviour – what we do).

Students: *explore* science content and contexts that matter to them; *interpret* opportunities and problems in the natural and physical worlds; *evaluate* the reliability and truthiness (validity) of scientific claims; *sort and report* issues in the natural and physical worlds; and *engage* in acts of citizenship in science contexts.

To explore what makes us curious – what we notice or measure – is one way of thinking like a scientist. Another way is to think about how we think about science: about observation, inference, testing and experimenting and, within this, about the need to verify, replicate and make predictions in many contexts. It is to be involved in an ongoing search for "temporary truths" that help us make sense of the world *and* an ongoing scrutiny of those temporary truths.

A scientific idea or theory about the natural and physical worlds can only ever be proved incorrect, not proved correct. It can be hard to understand the sense of temporary truth used when thinking like a scientist. For example, research shows that juries struggle when asked to interpret the significance of statistical scientific evidence that DNA found at a crime scene matches a suspect's DNA (Hans 2007).

If students are to think like a scientist, then they must learn to be comfortable about "temporary truths" – to develop the disposition to be open to the unknown, to the opportunity to revise, reorganise or change their ideas. They must also learn to think critically and creatively about the natural and physical worlds and the variables of influence in any given context.

At a certain point, student scientists who bring in ideas (researchers) must change focus and become student scientists who connect and extend ideas (decision-makers). The decisions can be made at an individual, community, national or global level. When scientists make decisions, they must be alert to (and actively look out for) unexpected consequences – they must look beyond what is known and be responsive to other ways of knowing in terms of both culture and discipline.

Science as human endeavour in the Australian Curriculum

In the Australian Science Curriculum (ACARA 2015), scientific research and decision-making is "thinking critically and creatively about our natural and physical world as human endeavour". The curriculum has a useful progression outlining how this thinking about how we think about science might be represented in a developmentally appropriate way using year levels as students move through:

- observing, asking questions and describing changes (Foundation, Years 1 and 2)
- making predictions and describing patterns and relationships (Years 3 and 4)
- testing predictions by gathering data and using evidence, and developing explanations of events and phenomena (Years 5 and 6)
- changing people's understanding, refining understanding as new evidence becomes available, and collaborating across disciplines and cultures (Years 7 and 8).

Any stage of the progression can be differentiated using SOLO levels (Exhibit 1.3).

Exhibit 1.3: Using SOLO levels to differentiate science as human endeavour (Foundation, Year 1 and Year 2)

	Unistructural	Multistructural	Relational	Extended abstract
• Observing • Asking questions • Describing changes	I need help to [xxx].	I can [xxx] if I am prompted.	I can [xxx] and I can explain how and why …	… **and** I can use my new learning to make predictions or find patterns or relationships.

Having the knowledge and skills to notice, infer and wonder about and test the reliability and validity of the theories used to explain everyday phenomena helps but is not enough to think like a scientist. You must also want to explore the natural and physical worlds in skilled and active ways – you must be ready, able and willing to think like a scientist.

New Zealand science capabilities

The New Zealand science capabilities or "ideas to think with" (Bull 2015) are similar to the Australian Curriculum's science as human endeavour. As "a set of ideas for teachers to think with" (Bull 2015), they help elaborate on the capacity and ability (capability) of being curious and thinking like a scientist. The capabilities integrate the New Zealand Curriculum key competencies with the science learning area notions of citizenship and the nature of science strand.

The science capabilities (Ministry of Education nd) are to:

- **gather and interpret data** – make careful observations and differentiate between observation and inference
- **use evidence** – support ideas with evidence and look for evidence supporting others' explanations
- **critique evidence** – appreciate that not all questions can be answered by science
- **interpret representations** – think about how data are presented and their effect on meaning (models, graphs, charts, diagrams and written texts)
- **engage with science** – use the capabilities above to engage with science in real-life contexts.

Science content and context

The capabilities provide a useful integrated framework for students and teachers imagining what it is like to think like a scientist about the natural and physical worlds and science itself. In addition, they encourage teachers to think about the NZC principle of **future focus** in ways that enable their students to develop Hayward's (2012) democratic imagination, motivation and involvement.

However, to provide opportunities for students to demonstrate, practise and assess progress against a science capability, teachers need to identify scientific content and context. A science capability cannot be developed in isolation. For example, the capability to gather and interpret data when studying congestion on a city motorway system will differ from the capability needed when gathering and interpreting data on fruit ripening in post-harvest crops, or core samples taken from deep within the alpine fault or species data on the diversity of marine species in an inner-city harbour.

What is the material world?

You know that we are living in a material world and I am a material girl.
(Madonna, "Material Girl", 1984)

In this book, we explore thinking like a scientist in the context of engaging with the material world. This means matter – the objects that surround us and the materials they are made from, such as metals, wood, glass, plastics and fabric.

Matter is the "stuff" of the universe – anything that has mass and takes up space. As we too take up space and have mass, we are matter. To spark a young person's scientific curiosity, simply take them outside to look at the night sky and tell them that "We're made of star stuff" (Cosmos TV Series, cited in Schrijver and Schrijver 2015). The atoms, molecules and ions that make up all matter (apart from hydrogen) originally came from the stars. Our bodies are made from the detritus from stars and the massive explosions in the galaxies – how cool is that?

Materials are the different types of matter that make up living things and objects. We use materials in all aspects of our lives, including as fuel, building materials, pharmaceuticals, clothing and cosmetics. Different types of matter differ in their properties (physical and chemical). Some properties are easily seen or measured. Others are only observed when materials are mixed, heated or cooled.

To understand the material world, students need to grasp the BIG science ideas or key understandings summarised in Exhibit 1.4 from the New Zealand and Australian curriculums.

Exhibit 1.4: Big ideas about the material world as described in the New Zealand and Australian curriculums

New Zealand Curriculum – Chemistry

- All matter is made of particles.
- The fundamental particle from which all matter is made is the atom.
- The properties of materials derive from the identity and arrangement of particles.
- Energy plays a key role in determining the changes that matter can undergo.
- Chemistry is everywhere.

Source: http://seniorsecondary.tki.org.nz/Science/Key-concepts/Key-concepts-Chemistry

Australian Curriculum – Chemical sciences

This sub-strand is concerned with understanding the composition and behaviour of substances.
- The chemical and physical properties of substances are determined by their structure at an atomic scale.
- Substances change and new substances are produced by rearranging atoms through atomic interactions and energy transfer.

Source: www.australiancurriculum.edu.au/science/structure

We suggest teachers prompt students to look for and make links to these big picture understandings when they are gathering and interpreting data (Exhibits 1.5 and 1.6).

Exhibit 1.5: HookED SOLO Describe++ triple strip map for BIG ideas in the material world

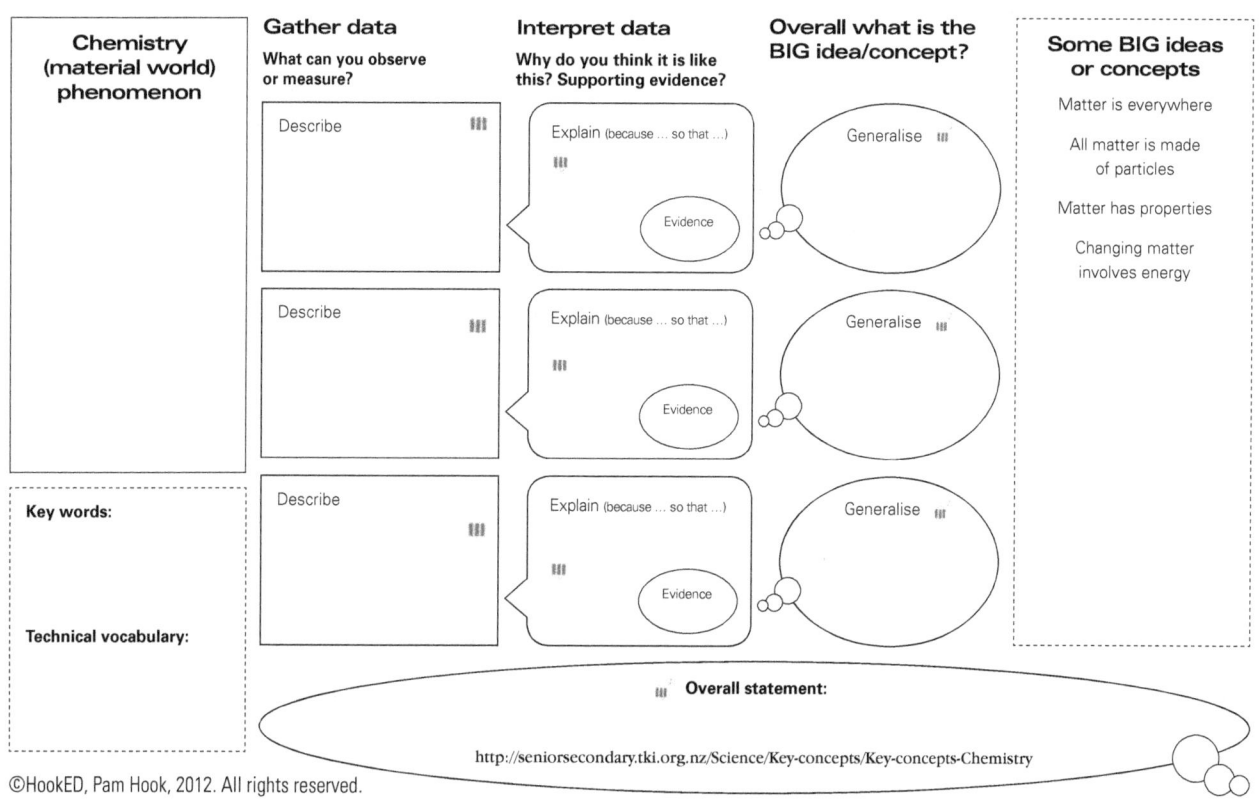

©HookED, Pam Hook, 2012. All rights reserved.

Exhibit 1.6: Applying SOLO to BIG ideas and understanding in the material world

Big idea 1: The universe is filled with "stuff" or "matter".

- Matter is anything that has mass and takes up space.
- Objects and materials have mass and take up space.
- Objects and materials are matter.

Unistructural	Multistructural	Relational	Extended abstract
Identify matter.	**Describe** matter using measures of mass and/or space.	**Classify** matter.	**Generalise** about matter.

Big idea 2: All matter is made of particles.

- All matter is made of discrete particles called atoms.
- Particles are in constant random motion.
- The space between particles is empty.
- Bonds or forces exist between particles.
- Approximately 115 different atoms form the building blocks of all known substances. Some of these atoms are more common than others.

Unistructural	Multistructural	Relational	Extended abstract
Identify matter in the form of a pure substance or a mixture.	Describe the particles making up a pure substance (element or compound) and/or a mixture (different elements and/or compounds).	Classify different samples of matter as pure substances or mixtures.	Generalise about the particles in properties of pure substances and mixtures.
Identify the states of matter: solid, liquid, gas.	Describe each state of matter. List the properties of each state of matter.	Explain causes for changes in state of matter in terms of space between particles.	Generalise about the changes of state of matter in terms of changes to the space between and movement of particles.
Identify some types of particles, eg, atoms, molecules, compounds, ions.	List the atoms in a particle, eg, water molecule contains hydrogen and oxygen atoms.	Analyse the formula of a substance, eg, water molecules (H_2O) are made up of two hydrogen atoms and one oxygen atom.	Generalise about the structure of particles, eg, water is a bent shape due to the two lone pairs of electrons around the oxygen atom, which repel the O–H bonds. This makes it a polar molecule.
Identify parts of the atom: electrons, protons, neutrons.	Describe an ion and an atom in terms of number and arrangement of electrons, protons and neutrons.	Explain the structure of an atom or ion. Compare and contrast atoms and ions of the same/different elements.	Justify (explain with evidence) how the structure of an atom/ion gives an element its unique properties/reactions.

continued ...

Exhibit 1.6: Applying SOLO to BIG ideas and understanding in the material world (continued)

Big idea 3: Matter has properties.
- Materials have observable properties.
- Properties are determined by the identity and arrangement of the particles (atoms) in the material.

Unistructural	Multistructural	Relational	Extended abstract
Identify a property of matter (a material).	Describe the properties of matter (a material).	Explain the properties of materials in terms of their particles and their arrangement.	Apply the properties of materials and the identity and arrangement of particles to the use of the material in everyday life.

Big idea 4: Changing matter involves energy. Since energy can be neither created nor destroyed, energy will determine the changes that matter can undergo.
- Materials can be changed.
- Changes to materials involve energy.
- Changes to materials can be reversible (physical change) or irreversible (chemical change).
- Change requires bonds between particles (atoms or molecules) to be broken and formed.
- Matter comes in different states – solid, liquid and gas.

Unistructural	Multistructural	Relational	Extended abstract
Identify signs of a change: • physical change (change of state) or • chemical reaction.	**Describe** the energy changes in: • a physical change (change of state) • a chemical reaction.	**Compare and contrast:** • a physical change with a chemical reaction • an exothermic reaction with an endothermic reaction.	**Generalise** about the energy changes in a chemical reaction or physical change.

Notes
Change of state: Easily reversed. No new substances formed. Heat must be added or removed.
Chemical reaction: Light generated, solid formed, gas produced, colour change, new substance formed.

How can SOLO help develop curious minds with the science capabilities?

As a beginning science teacher, I have found SOLO a really useful tool in making resources quickly and [it] allows students to understand the deeper concepts of the science capabilities.
(Science teacher, Lincoln High School)

The NZC essence statement for science (Ministry of Education 2007) describes students exploring and participating as critical, informed and responsible citizens. Students can be curious in both:

- **exploring** – by investigating and examining the natural physical world and how science itself works, or the extent to which the parts that comprise what we interpret as "science" contribute to the whole

- **participating** – by, as a critical citizen, evaluating for the common good; by, as an informed citizen interpreting or make meaning for the common good; and by, as a responsible citizen, adopting a "sort it or report it" attitude for the common good.

Exhibit 1.7 gives some examples of how SOLO helps make the different levels of demonstrating curiosity visible when exploring and participating.

Exhibit 1.7: SOLO levels for demonstrating curiosity when exploring and participating

SOLO level	Demonstrate curiosity when **exploring** the: • natural and physical worlds • matter • material world.	Demonstrate curiosity when **participating** as: • a critical citizen • an informed citizen • a responsible citizen.
Prestructural	I do not explore.	I do not take part.
Unistructural	I can explore if I am prompted, directed or shown what to do.	I can participate if I am prompted, directed or shown what to do.
Multistructural	I can explore but I am not certain about how or why this matters or even if I am exploring in the right ways.	I can participate but I am not certain about how or why this matters.
Relational	I can explore and I know how and why this matters ...	I can participate and I know how and why this matters ...
Extended abstract	... **and** my actions encourage others to explore the natural and physical worlds. Exploring is just part of who I am and what I do – I would be made uncomfortable if something or someone stopped me being curious about the material world.	... **and** my actions encourage others to participate as critical, informed, responsible citizens. Participating is just part of who I am and what I do – I would be made uncomfortable if something caused me to stop participating.

Furthermore the action verbs align to different levels of SOLO, as the discussion below elaborates. For example, *explore* is a surface-level task (prestructural, unistructural, multistructural), *interpret* is a deep-level task (relational) and *evaluate*, *sort and report*, *engage* are conceptual-level tasks (extended abstract).

Aligning the capabilities

SOLO can help identify the different levels of cognitive complexity in any task that includes the capabilities. So rather than aligning each science capability with a curriculum level or year level as in the Australian Curriculum example for science as human endeavour, we have aligned each science capability, which elaborates on what it is to think and act like a scientist (Ministry of Education nd), with its level of cognitive complexity using SOLO Taxonomy. For example:

- *gather data* and *interpret data* are SOLO multistructural and relational tasks
- *use evidence* is a SOLO relational task
- *critique evidence* is a SOLO extended abstract task
- *interpret representations* is a SOLO relational and extended abstract task
- *engage with science* is a SOLO extended abstract task.

Showing progress – assessing the capabilities

Assessing the capabilities, much like assessing the NZC key competencies, is not so straightforward. Do we assess knowledge, skills or attitudes related to the capabilities, or actual use of the capabilities in different contexts? Is the assessment of progress based on self-assessment, peer assessment, teacher assessment or some other measure of success? How should we deal with discrepancies between externally collected data and self-report data?

Because task and outcome can be at different levels of SOLO, we can use SOLO to differentiate the declarative (know about) and functioning (know how to) knowledge outcomes of each science capability. We can also assess changes in attitude towards thinking with the capabilities and changes in behaviour in deciding to demonstrate the capabilities. In this way we can construct SOLO-differentiated success criteria to show prior knowledge and progress in acquiring, consolidating and extending declarative and functioning knowledge of thinking with each science capability

Exhibit 1.8 shows one possible SOLO matrix for assessing the science capabilities. (For a detailed sample assessment, see page 65.)

Exhibit 1.8: SOLO self-assessment rubric for thinking like a scientist with the science capabilities

	Prestructural	Unistructural	Multistructural	Relational	Extended abstract
Knowing about the capabilities (declarative knowledge): Gather and interpret evidence, use evidence, critique evidence, interpret representations, engage in science	I have no ideas about [capability].	I can identify one idea about [capability].	I can describe several ideas about [capability] …	… **and** I can explain these ideas about [capability] …	… **and** I can make a generalisation about [capability].
Knowing how to demonstrate the capabilities (functioning knowledge): Gather and interpret evidence, use evidence, critique evidence, interpret representations, engage in science	I need help to demonstrate [capability].	I can demonstrate [capability] if prompted or directed.	I can demonstrate [capability] but am not certain about what I do.	I can demonstrate [capability] and explain how and why I do this.	I seek and act on advice on improving how I demonstrate [capability]. I am a role model for others.
Willingness to demonstrate the capabilities Disposition/attitude towards the science capabilities	I do not care about what or why things happen in the natural and physical worlds.	I pretend to care if the people around me show they think it is important.	Sometimes I think finding out more about the natural and physical worlds is important.	I think learning about how and why the natural and physical worlds work matters.	I would speak up if someone stopped others being curious about the natural and physical worlds.
Using the capabilities – how often? Behaviour – frequency of use in a given period, what students "do"	I never use the capabilities.	I use the capabilities once every couple of months.	I use the capabilities at least once a week.	I use the capabilities purposefully at least once a day.	I use the capabilities all day, every day as part of making sense of my world.
Using the capabilities – how flexibly? Behaviour – flexibility of what students "do"	Counting the flexibility of actual use (number of different capabilities used or perhaps the different places the capabilities are used – school, home – every day in every way) is more likely to interest a researcher.				
Using the capabilities – how consistently? Behaviour – consistency of what students "do" when the opportunity arises	Counting how consistently a capability is used each time the student engages in science.				

Notes
- For SOLO declarative knowledge and functioning knowledge rubric generators, go to: http://pamhook.com/solo-apps
- These capabilities are not fixed. Students will have different SOLO-level outcomes in different contexts and at different times.

Determining prior knowledge

SOLO Taxonomy is useful in helping determine the level of complexity of prior knowledge in:

- thinking like a scientist – how much do they know about thinking like a scientist and know how to think like a scientist?
- understanding the material world – how much do they know about the material world?

Finding out what the student already knows and can do (declarative knowledge and functioning knowledge) is important in planning activities that will enable all students to achieve the targeted outcome. Teaching what students already understand and/or what is beyond their immediate grasp is ineffective; it risks disengaging students from learning.

Some tools for determining prior knowledge strategies are surveys through discussions and continuums, SOLO Define and Describe maps and rubrics, SOLO hexagons and SOLO entry–exit tickets. Below is an overview of these approaches; for more details, see Hook (2016).

Survey (self-report) through discussion. Ask students to:

- pause – clear your mind and then think deeply about being a scientist
- discuss in a small group and then with the class the following question prompts in turn:
  - How do scientists think about the world?
  - Why do scientists think like this?
  - Have you ever thought like a scientist? What did you think about?
  - How do you feel when you are thinking like a scientist?
  - What do people need to know about thinking like a scientist?
  - How should we teach students to think like a scientist?
  - Why should we teach students to think like a scientist?
- record your answers to each question on a collaborative online document (eg, Google Docs) or Post-it notes and large sheets of newsprint
- curate your individual and group responses for future reference.

Survey (self-report) through continuums. Tell students that they will reflect on their attitude when thinking like a scientist using a values continuum. Set up the values continuum with opposing signs at each end, such as *Strongly agree – Strongly disagree*. Read out attitude statements (see suggestions in Exhibit 1.9) for students to respond to along the continuum.

Students can explain to others why they have chosen their position or they can pass if they wish. Emphasise that this activity is not a debate. Everyone's opinion is respected, as are everyone's reasons.

Exhibit 1.9: Suggestions for science attitude statements

I think …
- Science does more good than harm.
- It is important to know about science.
- We depend too much on science facts and information.
- Science is interesting.
- Scientists adjust their results to get the answers they want.
- Science makes people's lives change too fast.
- Science is unreliable – it has been wrong before.
- It is important to keep up to date on science issues.
- Jobs in science are very interesting.
- Science is boring.
- Science makes life easier for most people.
- Animals should not be used to test the effects of common materials on humans.
- Natural materials are better for you than synthetic materials.

Source: Built from:
British Science Association public attitudes to science (www.britishscienceassociation.org/public-attitudes-to-science-survey),
New Zealand public attitudes to science and technology survey (www.beehive.govt.nz/release/survey-reveals-kiwis-attitudes-science),
Pew Research Centre Report – public and scientists views on science and society (www.pewinternet.org/2015/01/29/public-and-scientists-views-on-science-and-society).

HOT SOLO Define map and rubric. Use these tools to determine prior knowledge before exploring thinking like a scientist.

How do I use them? See Hook and Mills (2011), page 30 and the instructional video, HookED SOLO Define Map Animation (**https://youtu.be/_iOvkCZCSAc**).

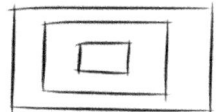

HookED SOLO hexagons. Teachers can use SOLO hexagons to determine prior knowledge and in formative and summative assessment (Exhibits 1.10 and 1.11). To this end, students generate ideas (and/or use teacher ideas), connect ideas, and then step back and make a generalisation (see Hook 2016, p 37).

Exhibit 1.10: SOLO hexagons at the different SOLO levels

Exhibit 1.11: Making links using SOLO hexagons

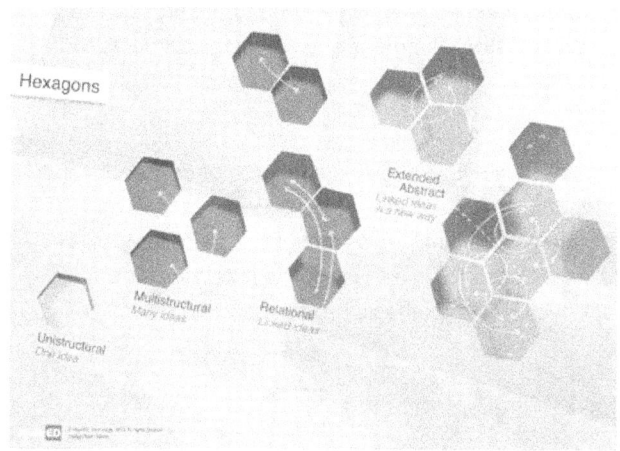

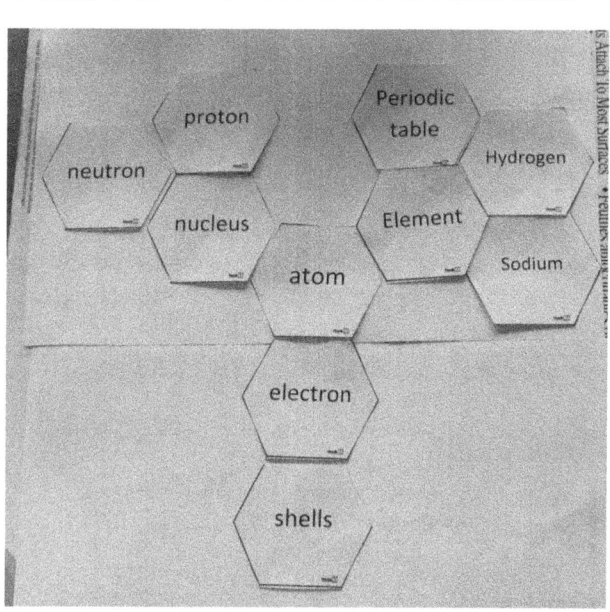

SOLO entry–exit tickets. Entry–exit tickets clearly identify what understanding students have gained over a given period. The entry ticket asks students to reflect on their prior knowledge about how well they demonstrate the science capabilities (Exhibit 1.12).

Exhibit 1.12: SOLO entry–exit ticket – demonstrating the science capabilities

Determining misconceptions (alternative conceptions)

Thinking like a scientist involves checking on and often "radically reorganising" the ideas and misunderstandings students have already learnt. This is important because students' enduring misconceptions or alternative conceptions undermine attempts to get them to think like scientists. They can prove very hard to shift. For example, research indicates that up to 40 per cent of 15-year-olds who have been taught about the particle model of matter still use their previous misconceptions in solving particle problems (Kind 2004).

After identifying such misconceptions, teachers must explicitly design learning experiences where students experience cognitive conflict, contradictions and counter-examples. It is not easy work. The following processes are useful in this task.

Process 1: Collaboration for dissent. After unpacking reasons for their thinking with others who hold similar views, students present their inferences and evidence to others with different perspectives. They listen to the presentations of groups with dissimilar views. Reflecting on this experience leads to the development of testable experiments to help establish or confront the point of view. Students consolidate the newly acquired knowledge by defending and using these new models.

For example, students explore a mystery substance like the non-Newtonian fluid oobleck (a mixture of cornstarch and water) as a way of confronting their existing conceptions of states of matter (see Box 1.1). They work in small groups: groups of those who believe the mixture is a solid and groups of those who think it is a liquid. Each group prepares a report on their inference for their point of view, giving reasons and evidence for it. They report on their findings and listen to the findings of all other groups. Finally groups rethink and test their hypothesis before reporting on any changes in their understanding (Exhibit 1.13).

Exhibit 1.13: Collaboration for dissent with SOLO levels differentiating task complexity

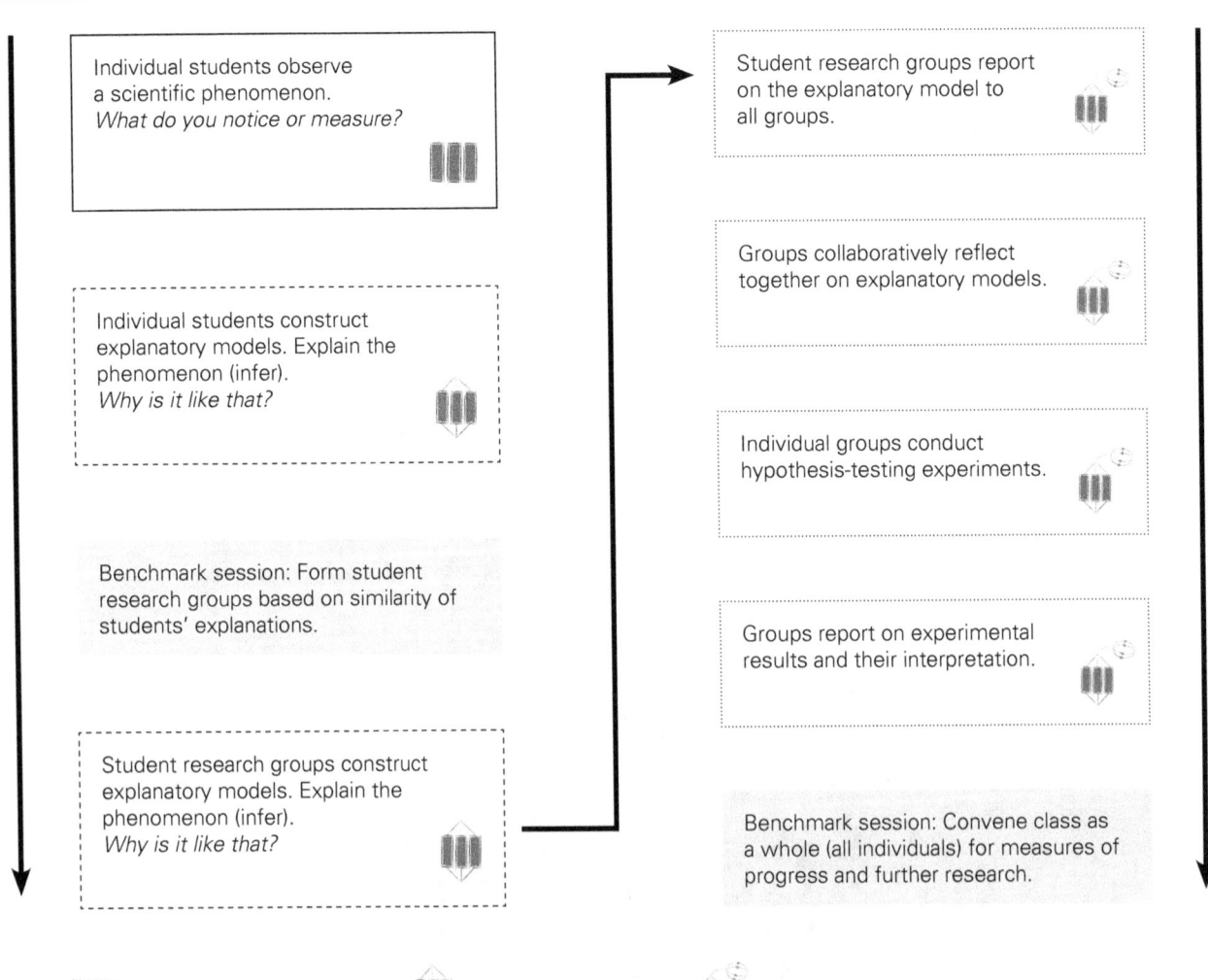

Key: SOLO multistructural   SOLO relational   SOLO extended abstract

Source: Adapted from Oshima et al (2004)

Process 2: Self-repair read aloud. In an alternative approach, students "self-repair" their misconceptions when they are prompted to explain a text aloud to themselves as they read (Chi 2000). This task uses SOLO relational level connectives like *because* and *so that*.

> **Box 1.1: Student misconceptions and alternative conceptions**
>
> Some common misconceptions among students are that:
>
> - solids are hard and rigid so materials like jelly, plasticine and sand cannot be solids because they are not hard or rigid enough and lack a definite shape (Kind 2004; Smolleck and Hershberger 2011; Stavy and Stachel 1985)
> - mass and weight are the same. Yet mass is a measure of how much "matter" is in an object and remains constant, while weight is a measure of the force of gravity pulling on an object so can change depending on whether you are on earth or the moon or floating in space. From this misconception come significant misconceptions about change of state
> - melting matter, as in melting in ice, makes it lighter. Students do not conserve the number of particles in a solid and liquid when the solid becomes a liquid (Gabel et al 1987)
> - when you add heat energy to water, the bubbles in boiling water are air, oxygen or hydrogen, or heat rather than bubbles of water in a vapour state (steam)
> - gases do not have mass (Stavy 1990a, 1990b). Students infer that a blown-up balloon has the same mass as a deflated one and that ice molecules weigh more than water vapour molecules
> - when a solute (a soluble solid) dissolves in a solvent (a liquid) and disappears, it ceases to exist and the weight of the solution remains the same as the original solvent
> - air does not contain water in a gaseous state. So students fail to appreciate that gaseous water in air will change to water in a liquid state if heat energy is removed
> - when water in a shallow container is left to evaporate and the volume reduces, the water is absorbed by the walls of the container, vanishes, dries up or changes into air. Students do not infer that the water in the container is simply changing state from a liquid to a gas
> - water is the only liquid that exists. They exclude shampoo, tomato sauce, honey, smoothie, cooking oil and so on
> - solids are the only forms of matter – liquids are not matter as they have nothing in common with solids, and gases are not matter because you cannot see them
> - air does not "exist" because it cannot be seen or smelled
> - air and oxygen are the same thing
> - particles of matter possess properties that we associate with macroscopic matter. For example, gold atoms are shiny and hard, or water molecules are tiny droplets
> - air does not occupy space
> - ice is a different substance from water
> - ice floating in water means all solid objects will float in any liquid
> - the amount of water increases when it is frozen (due to ice expansion)
> - matter expands due to the expansion of the individual particles, rather than the increase in spacing between particles
> - all liquids mix
> - all metals are magnetic.
>
> Note: The United States National Science Teachers Association has developed *Uncovering Student Ideas in Science* (vols 1–4), a series of powerful formative assessment probes that help teachers identify the misconceptions students hold. Search for it at: www.nsta.org

Identifying developmentally appropriate content and ideas in the material world

After a teacher has identified students' prior knowledge, both teacher and students can use SOLO to assess and self-assess next steps. To be developmentally appropriate, content should sit approximately at a (+1) SOLO level advance on the student's current level of understanding. Exhibit 1.14 shows one approach to aligning next steps in learning in a developmentally appropriate way.

Exhibit 1.14: Example of developmentally appropriate next steps, advancing by SOLO level +1

NZC Science: Material world: Properties and changes of matter		
Levels 1 and 2: *Observe, describe* and *compare* physical and chemical properties of common materials and changes that occur when materials are mixed, heated or cooled.	**Levels 3 and 4:** *Group* materials in different ways, based on the observations and measurements of the characteristic chemical and physical properties of a range of different materials. *Compare* chemical and physical changes.	**Level 5:** *Investigate* the chemical and physical properties of different groups of substances, for example, acids and bases, fuels and metals. *Distinguish* between pure substances and mixtures and between elements and compounds.
Example next steps by SOLO level		
Multistructural: *observe, describe* Relational: *compare* Do all materials behave the same way when heated? Observe physical and chemical changes. Heat a variety of substances (eg, wax, ice, wood, paper, copper carbonate). Describe how some materials change their state (physical change) and others undergo a chemical reaction (chemical change).	Relational: *group (classify), compare* Classify examples. Physical changes are temporary and relatively easy to undo. For example, a metal lid on a glass jar expands when heated; water (l) changes to water (s) when heat energy is removed. Chemical changes are permanent and hard to undo. For example, burning changes wood to charcoal and ash; cooking an egg changes the runny, clear albumen to firm, opaque white. Particle arrangement changes in both physical and chemical changes but in a chemical change the particles themselves are changed.	Multistructural: *investigate* Relational: *distinguish between* Explore elemental samples. Teacher presents demo or video of poisonous and dangerous elements. Research properties of metals and non-metals. Locate the groupings of metals and non-metals on the periodic table. Relate position on periodic table to metal reactivity. Use models to compare and contrast particle arrangement in pure substances and mixtures and between elements and compounds.

Properties	Add heat →	Properties	Physical change
Common material (before)	Remove heat →	Common material (after)	
Particles	Mix →	Particles	Chemical change

When students are learning about the material world, they have the advantage of being familiar in an everyday sense with plastics such as polythene, synthetic rubbers, fibres such as cotton, metals, glass and wood. Prior knowledge and engagement provide great content for curious exploration, science research, experimentation and decision-making about waste management in the material world. In exploring the wicked problems and conflicting beliefs about waste management in their local communities, students gain many developmentally appropriate opportunities for learning to think like a scientist and developing the science capabilities, within the NZC nature of science and material world strands.

2. Gather and interpret data

Learners make careful observations and differentiate between observation and inference in the material world. (NZC science capability, Ministry of Education nd)

The distinction between gathering data and interpreting data is important when thinking like a scientist:

- To **gather data**, scientists make specific, detailed observations and measurements of a scientific phenomenon.
- To **interpret data**, they explain these observations by making inferences. Inferences may or may not be correct. For example, if we observe vigorous bubbling after adding vinegar to baking soda, we may infer the bubbles are carbon dioxide gas released during the reaction between an acid and a carbonate. It would be incorrect to claim we observed carbon dioxide gas being given off because we did not test the nature of the gas bubbles given off.

You can build student curiosity and understanding about this distinction with "observation and inference mystery bags". Each opaque bag contains an object made from the material world. Students make observations without seeing the object but using their other senses (and recording them on a record sheet such as Exhibit 2.1). Then, using their observations, they make inferences about the contents of each bag. Finally, they open the bags to check their inferences against the contents.

Exhibit 2.1: Sample of record sheet for observation and inference mystery bags

Mystery object number	What do you notice?	What do you infer?	What is the actual object?

Gathering data (multistructural level)

Gathering data is a SOLO multistructural task. We think like a scientist when we are curious about and notice (and/or measure) the small stuff in our lives, and when we demonstrate the capability to gather data from direct (or indirect) observations of what is happening around us.

Matter

In the material world we might ask students to gather data when on a walk in their local environment spotting metal, plastics, wood, fibre and glass or when we pass around samples of matter (eg, wood, iron, polystyrene, cork). We ask them to gather data about matter (Exhibit 2.2). What can they observe or measure? How much data can they collect? When handling samples of matter we ask how heavy the blocks feel. What is "heavy"? What is "hard"? Can they rank the samples in order of how heavy or how hard they feel? Do they know the science term for heaviness? If we give them a bucket of water, can they gather data on the floating and sinking behaviours of the objects (matter) in water?

Exhibit 2.2: "Gather data" questions

What did you hear?	What did you notice?	How hard is it?
What did you see?	What did you measure?	How heavy is it?
What did you smell?	What colour is it?	How bright is it?
What did you feel?	What temperature is it?	How quickly did it dissolve?

Becoming curious about floating and sinking requires more data. With data on the densities (g/cm^3) of different materials, including water, students can explore further, comparing the densities of objects that float in water with those that sink and then compare this discovery with the density of water. When these materials are not useful any more and end up in rivers, lakes or the ocean, will they float or sink? Can students rank the materials on Mohs scale (showing relative hardness)? Use other properties of matter to further classify matter into groups like plastic, wood and metal. Explore the environment further to find examples of how these common materials are used, where they came from and how they are disposed of.

States of matter

Matter occurs in different states. In primary school we usually limit our descriptors to solids, liquids and gases.[2] To introduce solids and liquids, take students on a slow walk across the campus. Acting as "material world forensic scientists", they will surprise themselves in exploring (locating, identifying, observing and inferring about) many everyday examples. You can explore gases as "moving air" or wind, when inflating balloons or blowing bubbles in dishwashing liquid, in carbonated soft drinks, or as seen stored in cylinders such as in a car workshop or doctor's surgery.

Exhibit 2.3: Gathering data in summary

To **gather data** (SOLO multistructural task) is to notice and/or measure science phenomena. Students need scientific language to help them talk about what they observe, such as language for variables, units, common materials and states of matter.	Examples of tasks: Identify common materials. Describe their properties and everyday uses. Explore how common materials (solids, liquids or gases) change when they are mixed, heated or cooled. Look for indicators of physical and chemical change: change of colour; change in temperature or energy – production (exothermic) or loss (endothermic) of heat; change of form; change in pH; giving off light, heat or sound; formation of gases, often appearing as bubbles; formation of precipitate (insoluble particles); decomposition of organic matter

Students can self-assess how well they can gather data using a SOLO functioning knowledge rubric (Exhibit 2.4) and how well they can talk about the data they gather using a SOLO declarative knowledge rubric (Exhibit 2.5).

Exhibit 2.4: SOLO self-assessment rubric for functioning knowledge about gathering reliable, accurate, valid data

Gathering data about the material world	Prestructural	Unistructural	Multistructural	Relational	Extended abstract
Functioning knowledge (how to)	I need help to gather data about the material world.	I can gather data about the material world if I copy someone else.	I can gather data about the material world but am unsure if they are relevant.	I can gather data about the material world and explain why they are relevant.	I can seek and act on feedback to improve the ways I gather data.
Essential strategies	Build scientific vocabulary	Repeat observations and measurements to increase reliability.	Check for errors and control variables to increase accuracy and validity.		

Exhibit 2.5: SOLO self-assessment rubric for declarative knowledge about gathering reliable, accurate, valid data

Gathering data about the material world	Prestructural	Unistructural	Multistructural	Relational	Extended abstract
Declarative knowledge (knowing about)	I need help to gather relevant data about the material world.	I can gather one piece of data about the material world.	I can gather several pieces of data about the material world.	I can gather data about the material world and explain why they are relevant.	I can seek and act on feedback to improve the relevance of the data I have gathered.
Essential strategies	Build scientific vocabulary			"because", "so that"	

---

2   The other two known states of matter are plasma and Bose-Einstein condensates.

Science vocabulary

To gather data, students need to be fluent in a rich scientific language. They need terms and units to identify the variables scientists use such as for distance, time, speed, acceleration, mass, force, energy, work and power. In studying the material world, students need to know words like *solid, liquid, gas, metal, plastic, wood, glass, mixture, dissolve, condense, sublime*. (See page 23 on using SOLO hexagons to build a science glossary.) Students can use a SOLO rubric to self-assess their ability to use science language (Exhibit 2.6).

Exhibit 2.6: SOLO self-assessment rubric for using scientific language in relation to a scientific observation

Functioning knowledge	Prestructural	Unistructural	Multistructural	Relational	Extended abstract
Using scientific terms Examples: *solid, liquid, gas, metal, wood, glass, plastic, rubber, textile*	I need help to use science terms for common materials and their properties.	I can use science terms for common materials and their properties if directed.	I can use science terms for common materials and their properties but I make mistakes. I do not know why or when to use them or how to correct my mistakes.	I use science terms for common materials and their properties in my science writing and conversation. I know why and when to use them.	I seek feedback on how to use science terms to clarify my scientific writing and conversation. I can help others use them to express scientific ideas.

Interpreting data (relational level)

Interpretation is a SOLO relational task. It is not enough for scientists to simply notice (and/or measure); they must also make meaning – interpret data and make inferences about what they have seen. This task involves deeper thinking because a student must hold on to the data in their working memory and then integrate the data to interpret them in different ways by making links between the new data and what they have seen and their previous experience of the world. To make these links, students use connectives like *because* and *so that*.

Asking "why?" builds curious minds. Repeatedly asking "why?" helps create an expectation for interpreting or making meaning. Relational-level questions that build curiosity and interpretation skills prompt students to make meaning – such as to explain why and how, and to find order, groups, subgroups, similarities, differences and analogies (Exhibit 2.7).

Exhibit 2.7: "Interpret data" questions

What is the order?	What are the parts?	Why do you think it is like that?
What group does it belong to?	How do the parts influence the whole?	What does this remind you of?
What is the cause?	What did you feel?	What can you infer?
What is the consequence?	What is it like?	How does this relate to …?
Why did it happen?	How is it different?	
How did it happen?	How is it similar?	

For example, students are made curious about the data they collect on the density and floating and sinking behaviour of common materials when we ask them to interpret other seemingly conflicting data on floating and sinking:

> What does it mean when different fruits and vegetables sink or float when placed in water? What happens when we add ice cubes to a glass of water? Is ice more or less dense than water? Can you infer why an unpeeled orange floats but a peeled orange sinks? Why do most of us float in water but sharks sink if they stop swimming? Does fat float or sink in water? Can you explain how and why fatbergs clog underground sewers?

Students use unexpected results to revise and extend this thinking and to revisit and re-puzzle over the many different properties that make plastics useful in their everyday life:

> Will plastic debris float or sink in the ocean? Why are patches of floating plastic materials in the ocean hard to spot? Where does plastic ocean debris come from? What happens to the plastic microbeads in face scrubs? What should we do when up to 10 per cent of the world's plastic ends up in the oceans?

Exhibit 2.8: Interpreting data in summary

To interpret data (SOLO relational task) is to make connections between what is observed and our previous knowledge and experience. We use these connections to make inferences about what we notice or measure. **To make connections** (SOLO relational task) is to sequence, classify, compare and contrast, explain cause and effect and/or analyse what is noticed.	Examples of tasks: Make connections: between properties and uses; between properties and natural occurrences; based on similar properties; based on what happens when common materials are mixed, heated or cooled.

Students can self-assess how well they can interpret data from the material world using a SOLO functioning knowledge rubric (Exhibit 2.9) and how well they can talk about their interpretations using a SOLO declarative knowledge rubric (Exhibit 2.10).

Exhibit 2.9: SOLO self-assessment rubric for functioning knowledge about interpreting data

Interpreting data about the material world	Prestructural	Unistructural	Multistructural	Relational	Extended abstract
Functioning knowledge (how to) Use relational-level verbs	I need help to interpret data about the material world.	I can interpret data about the material world if I copy someone else.	I can interpret data about the material world but am unsure if they are correct.	I can interpret data about the material world and explain their relevance.	I can seek and act on feedback to improve the ways I interpret data.

Exhibit 2.10: SOLO self-assessment rubric for declarative knowledge about interpreting data

Interpreting data about the material world	Prestructural	Unistructural	Multistructural	Relational	Extended abstract
Declarative knowledge (know about) Use relational-level verbs	I need help to interpret data about the material world.	I can make one interpretation about material world data.	I can make several interpretations about material world data …	… and I can give reasons why my interpretations are relevant …	… and I can seek and act on feedback to improve how I interpret data.

Progress when thinking with the capability "gather and interpret data"

When we think with the capability "gather and interpret data", we ask:

- What do I know about gathering and interpreting data? What is it? What is it like? *Declarative knowledge*
- How well do I know how to gather and interpret data (directed, supported, independent use)? *Functioning knowledge – skill*
- How likely am I to gather and interpret data? *Attitude – will*
- How frequently (how often) do I gather and interpret data? *Behaviour*
- How flexibly (in different contexts, with different methods) do I gather and interpret data? *Behaviour*

Students can show progress in any or all of the above. The next section offers a range of strategies to support this progress.

Strategies for gathering and interpreting data

In this section we share examples of learning strategies (including SOLO maps and rubrics) for exploring the science capability "gather and interpret data" as an idea to think with in the content and context of the material world.

Going for a common materials walk in the local community

To help students identify and explore everyday examples of different materials and the properties that make them useful, simply go on a walk and gather data from a place in the local community such as a supermarket or adventure playground. As "common material" forensic scientists, they might identify metals (eg, copper, iron, brass, aluminium) and non-metals (eg, plastic, wood, rubber, ceramics, organic polymers). Then challenge students to dig deeper and explain the properties they used to identify the material.

Distinguishing objects from materials is important if students are to think like scientists but they often confuse the two (Rutledge 2010). *Material* describes "stuff" – what an *object* is made of. For example, a shiny, sharp scissor blade (object) is made of a metal (material). To address this confusion, take care in how you talk about "materials" with students, and play games such as "What is the object made of …?" and "I spy an object" vs "I spy a material".

Also important is developing a rich science vocabulary related to properties (Exhibit 2.11). Such a vocabulary will enhance students' observations of common materials like metals in their local environment and help them to avoid confusing descriptors like *smooth–soft* and *hard–strong*. Games like "Odd one out" are helpful ways of introducing and building on scientific language. See also Exhibit 2.6 above for a SOLO self-assessment rubric for using scientific language.

Exhibit 2.11: Sample of useful scientific language for properties of materials

transparent	opaque	translucent	strong	weak
soft	waterproof	absorbent	flexible	rigid
magnetic	conductor (heat)	insulator (heat)	insulator (electricity)	malleable
ductile	shiny	dull	elastic	plasticity
melts easily	rough	smooth	hard	burns easily (flammable)
burns when heated	melts when heated	dissolves in water	can be poured	viscous

On the walk, students can track the different materials the class uses across a day or during a favourite recreational activity or with a technological device. They will initially focus on materials in their solid state as it is hard for students to think like a scientist about liquids (apart from water) and gases (see Box 1.1 in section 1 above). Stavy (1988) suggests that deliberate acts of instruction are needed for students to know about gases.

Using a SOLO self-assessment rubric (Exhibit 2.12), students can self-assess their ability to observe and infer on the walk.

Further exploration and guided inquiry after the walk will reveal that materials can be changed and that these changes are often prompted by adding or removing heat or when materials are combined (mixed) with other materials. At this stage students will notice that some changes are reversible (physical) and some are not – they are irreversible and represent chemical change.

Using HookED SOLO hexagons

> *SOLO hexagons allow my students to go beyond basic understanding of concepts and allow them to visualise the links between ideas and explore the dynamic nature of science.* (Science teacher, Lincoln High School)

The SOLO hexagons activity prompts students to make connections and interpret (think more deeply about) data or science ideas. Using different-coloured paper for different groups of hexagons (eg, different colours for solids, liquids and gases or for different types of common materials) helps further differentiate the material world content.

Exhibit 2.12: SOLO self-assessment rubric for gathering and interpreting data on a common materials walk

Functioning knowledge	**Prestructural**	**Unistructural**	**Multistructural**	**Relational**	**Extended abstract**
Gather and interpret data Learners make careful observations and differentiate between observation and inference on a common materials walk.	I need help to gather and interpret data on the walk. I do not know how what I observe and measure differs from what I infer from my observations and measurements.	I can gather data on the walk if prompted or directed. I can interpret data on the walk if I am prompted or directed.	I can gather data on the walk and interpret the data but I am not sure about what I am doing (trial and error – aware of strategies but not sure why or when to use them).	I can gather data on the walk and interpret data and explain why they are relevant (strategic or purposeful use of strategies – know why and when to use them).	I can teach others to gather and/or interpret data. I can evaluate how to improve the way I gather and interpret data. I can gather and/or interpret data about the material world in other settings.
Effective strategies (add teacher and student suggestions)	What can you see? Why do you think it is like that?			HookED SOLO Describe++ map and rubric	

In doing this activity, as well as making connections between states of matter, particle models, properties and uses of common materials collected on individual hexagons, students practise and develop using scientific language. They need explicit support to become familiar with scientific language, which can be quite daunting. For example, even for observing something as simple as mixing solids in liquids, the science vocabulary with its overabundance of "s" words can be very confusing:

> A *solid* that dissolves in water is a *solute* and water is the *solvent*. The *solute* and *solvent* make up a *solution*. The *solution* can be dilute or concentrated, *saturated* or unsaturated. If a *solid* added to water *settles* out, you have a *suspension*.

Building a SOLO hexagons science glossary is a powerful way to give students the working vocabulary they need to think like a scientist. To extend the hexagon activity, place definitions on the reverse side of the hexagons to reinforce science language and clarify how to use it (Exhibit 2.13).

Exhibit 2.13: Building science vocabulary when using SOLO hexagons

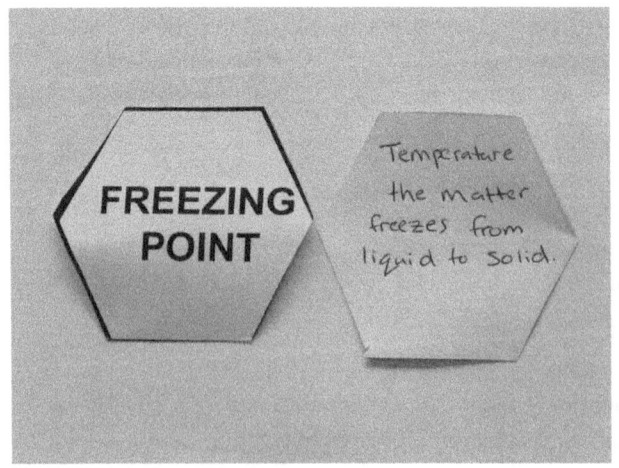

a. With definitions

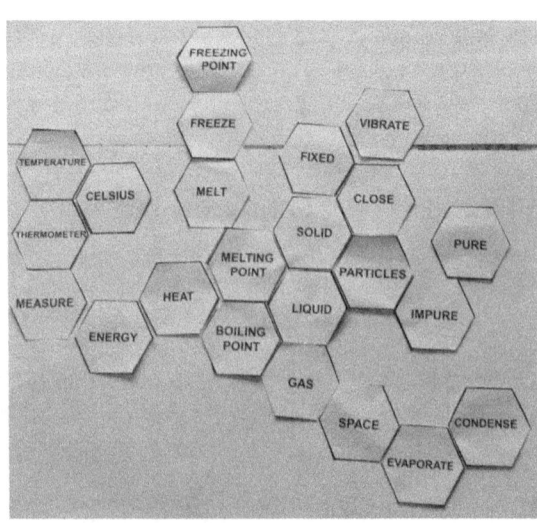

b. With explanations

Using the HOT SOLO Describe map and rubric

The HOT SOLO Describe map and self-assessment rubric prompt deep thinking when gathering and interpreting data. They support students to identify the attributes or characteristics of an idea or object using adjectives and adjectival phrases.

How do I use them? See Hook and Mills (2011), page 33 and the instructional video, HookED SOLO Describe Map Animation (**https://youtu.be/5IHuzj4-z-0**).

Relevant tasks: Describe. What is it like? A HOT SOLO Describe map (and rubric) can build student literacy outcomes when they are describing outcomes like:

- properties of states of matter (Exhibit 2.14 – note this example still includes some of the student's "temporary truths" that could be tested through conducting experiments that the student either designs independently or co-constructs with the teacher) or common materials (Exhibit 2.15)
- effects of heating, cooling or mixing on common materials
- reversible or irreversible change.

Variations on this map include the HookED SOLO strip map and the HookED SOLO Describe++ map and rubric described in the following subsections.

Properties of common materials. Students develop a surface understanding of the material world when they ask:

- What is the object?
- What material is it made of?
- What are its properties?
- What are its physical properties?
- What are its chemical properties?

When students act like forensic scientists, they observe, describe and compare the different materials used in objects like the specialist uniform and equipment used by workers in the local community (eg, ambulance officers, shearers, commercial fishers, fencers, takeaway outlet workers, caretakers, fire officers, police officers, carpenters, mechanics).

Once they can confidently identify materials and describe their properties, they can connect their ideas by asking:

- Why is this material suitable?
- How are these properties similar to those in other materials?
- How else do we use this material?
- Where did it come from?
- How did it get to be like it is?

They can even extend this thinking to wonder about what happens to all this stuff when we don't want it any more:

- How do we get rid of this material – can we ever really get rid of it if the atoms still exist?
- How do we manage this material when we want to throw it away?

Distinguishing between an object and a material. Students often need help to distinguish between use of an object and the property of a material. For example, when you blow into a balloon, they may claim the "balloon" stretches to let more air in rather than that the property of the material the balloon is made of, rubber (stretchiness), lets the air in. Using a SOLO Describe map focused on the materials can help students distinguish between properties of the material and properties of an object.

Different properties can help explain why a particular material is used in an object. For example, you might ask students to infer why a material like merino wool fabric was chosen for flight attendant uniforms or why metals are used in saucepans (Exhibit 2.15). Students can use this thinking about materials and their properties to perform their own investigations into the most suitable materials for a task they want to successfully complete (eg, mopping up a spilled drink, blocking sun glare in a classroom, exfoliating human skin).

Exhibit 2.16 gives an example of a SOLO Describe rubric for self-assessing a description of the properties of a common material. This rubric has been co-constructed between teacher and students.

Exhibit 2.14: HOT SOLO Describe map with prompts to describe the properties of a solid

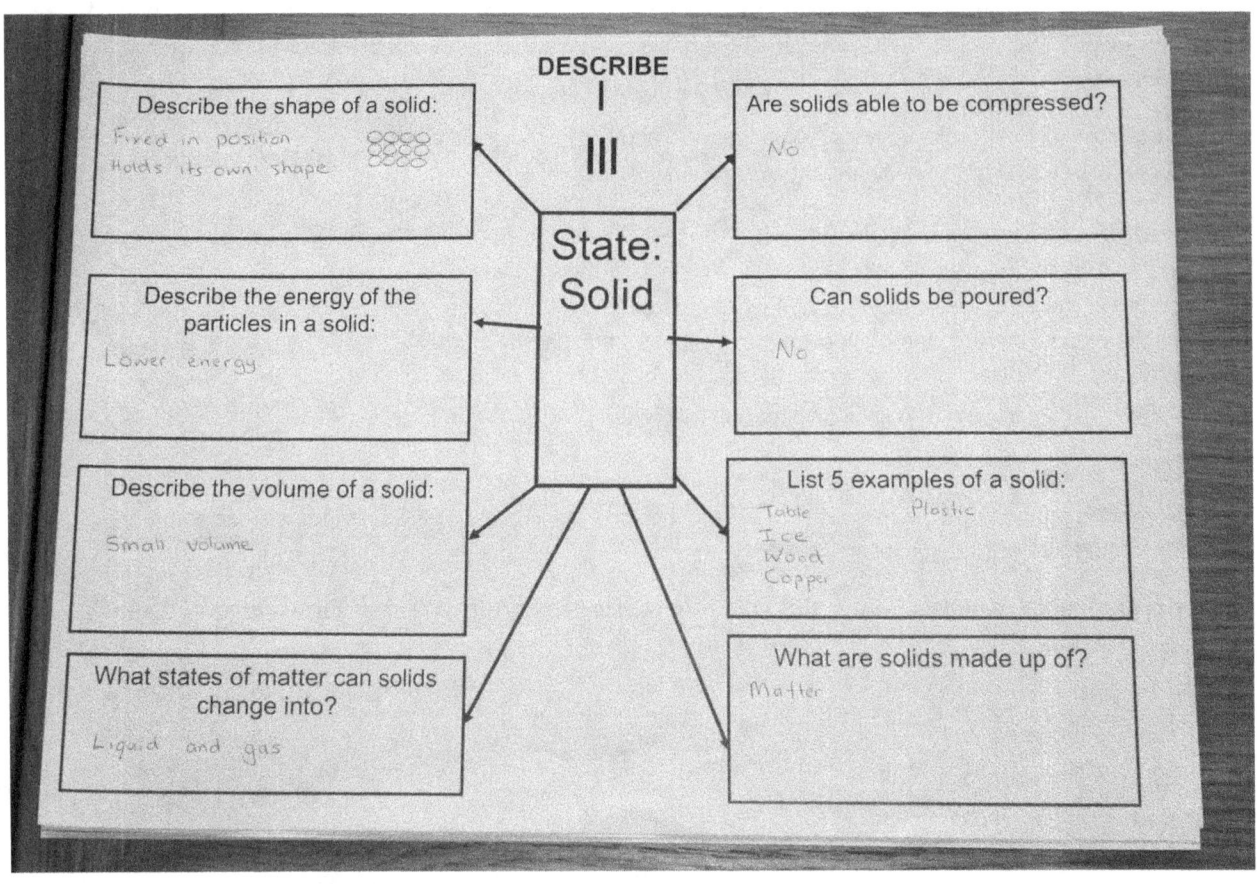

Exhibit 2.15: HOT SOLO Describe map with inference prompts to describe properties of metals

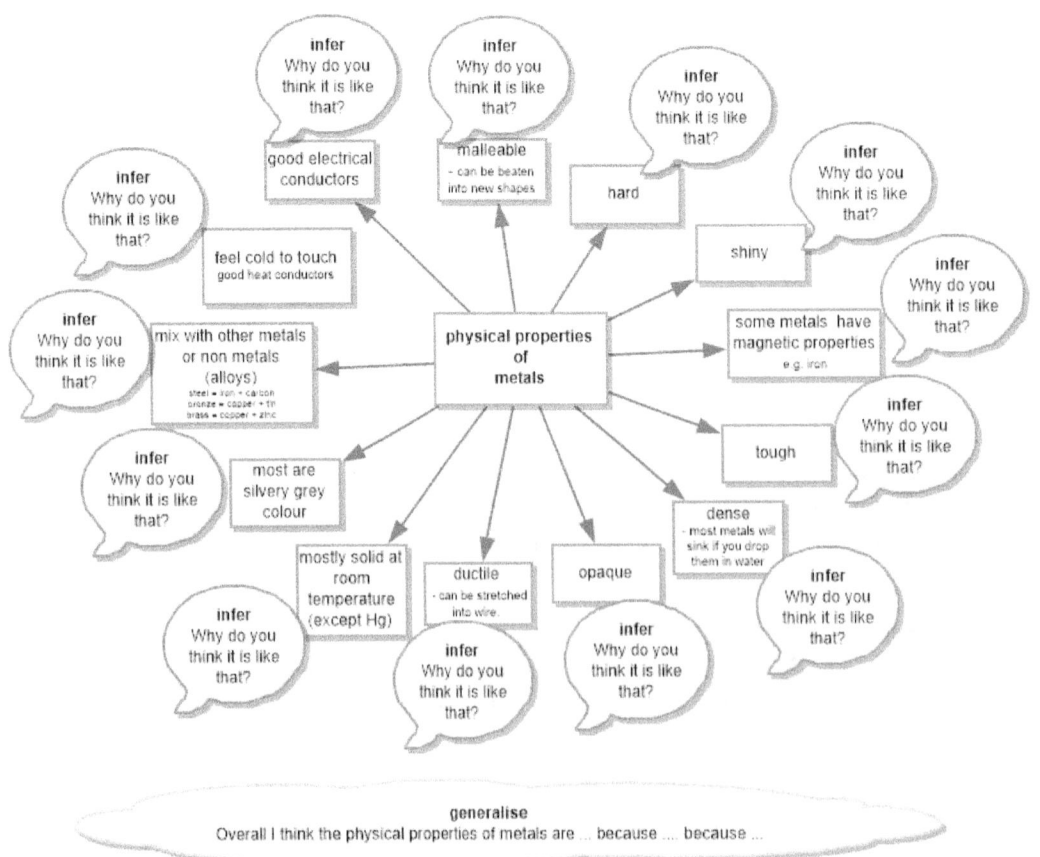

Exhibit 2.16: HOT SOLO Describe self-assessment rubric for describing common materials

	Prestructural	Unistructural	Multistructural	Relational	Extended abstract
Describe an object in terms of its common material (metal, wood, plastic).	I need help to identify an object.	I can identify an object.	I can describe an object by its common materials – what it is made of.	I can compare and contrast two objects on the basis of their common materials.	I can sort objects on the basis of their materials.
Describe properties of common materials (hard, strong, bendy, soft, cold, shiny, heavy, flexible, weak, soft).	I need help to identify a property of a common material.	I can identify a property of a common material. I can identify solids and liquids.	I can describe the properties of a common material. I can describe the properties of solids, liquids and gases.	I can compare and contrast the properties of different materials, and solids, liquids and gases.	I can sort materials based on their properties and can classify a range of solids, liquids and gases.
Describe the uses of common materials.	I need help to identify the use of a common material.	I can identify the use of a common material.	I can describe the uses of common materials …	… **and** I can relate the use to each material's properties …	… **and** I can predict its use from its properties.
Effective strategies *(add teacher and student suggestions)*					

Using the HookED SOLO strip map

The HookED SOLO strip map is a strategy for deep description as an alternative to the HOT SOLO Describe map. It works well with young learners who might be overwhelmed by the complete map and also to prompt deep thinking when older students work collaboratively, with each student taking responsibility for completing a separate strip.

How do I use it? See Hook (2016), page 48.

Relevant tasks: Describe, infer, wonder. What do you notice/measure? Why is it like that? What can you infer? What does it make you wonder? These question prompts for surface (SOLO multistructural), deep (SOLO relational) and conceptual (SOLO extended abstract) understanding all feature in the HookED SOLO strip map (Exhibit 2.17).

Exhibit 2.17: HookED SOLO strip map

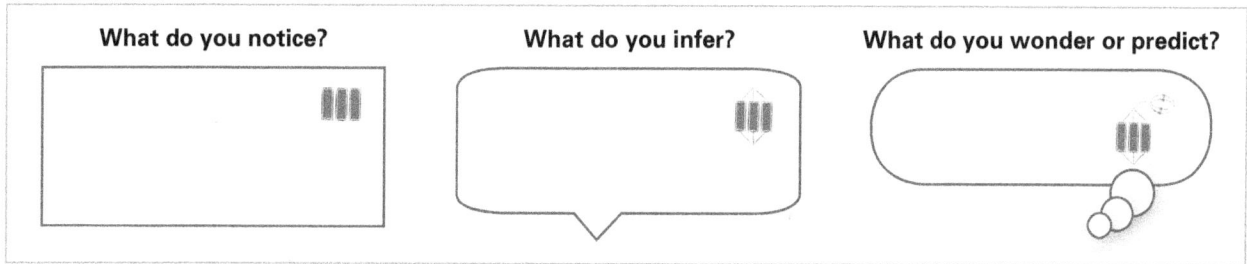

Any everyday life experience of (and with) common materials will deepen students' understanding of the nature of the materials and their properties – a SOLO multistructural task. The aim of asking why certain materials are suited for particular tasks is to deepen understanding through connecting ideas. For example, students can investigate samples of different materials and explore how their properties help explain their use in different contexts (eg, in sporting equipment, mobile phones, packaging, building structures, smart sensors and occupational uniforms). To extend this understanding to another context, we can ask students what the connection makes them wonder.

The following examples show how to use this strategy to describe properties of carbon fibre reinforced polymers (Exhibit 2.18) and, using a three-level format, to describe a mobile phone's materials and their properties (Exhibit 2.19).

Exhibit 2.18: HookED SOLO strip map to describe properties of carbon fibre reinforced polymers

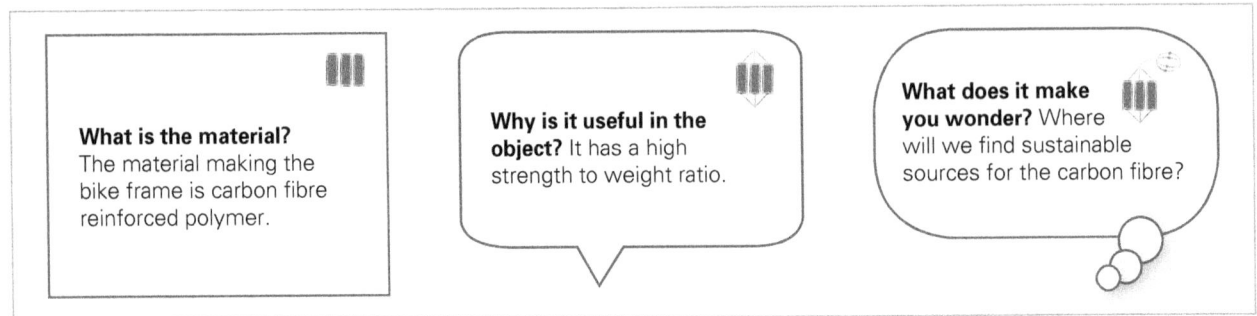

Exhibit 2.19: HookED SOLO strip map using three levels to describe a mobile phone's materials and their properties

Bringing in ideas			Connecting ideas	Extending ideas
SOLO multistructural			SOLO relational	SOLO extended abstract
Observe	Identify	Describe	Infer	Wonder
What can you see? What can you measure?	What is it made of (material/s)? Give examples	What are the properties of the material/s?	Why do you think (infer) this material is used in the object?	What does it make you wonder?
Mobile phone	Metals (40%), eg, copper in wiring and transistors, cobalt in lithium batteries	High conductivity	Is useful to enhance electron flow in the circuit board	What are alternatives to using copper in circuits? What are environmental and social costs of mining for metals – how and where is cobalt mined?
	Plastics (40%), eg, polycarbonate plastic in the casing	High-impact resistance	Is useful to protect the phone from damage during use	When will our bodies become wearable casings for mobile technologies in the future?
	Glass, eg, aluminosilicate glass in the touch screen	Toughened to resist shattering or scratching, transparent	Protects the touch screen from damage	How will screen quality (transparency) and conductivity improve?

When students collaborate sharing their SOLO strip map thinking, they construct multi-strip versions of the HookED SOLO Describe++ map. These multi-strip maps help protect student thinking – capturing each flow of ideas from surface to deep thinking in a different strand and in this way providing a collaborative resource template to write or talk from (see below).

Using the HookED SOLO Describe++ map and rubric

The HookED SOLO Describe++ map and self-assessment rubric prompt deep thinking when gathering and interpreting data. They identify the attributes or characteristics of an idea or object using adjectives and adjectival phrases and then take each of these ideas deeper using prompts for relational and extended abstract thinking.

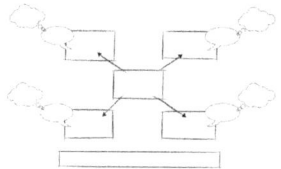

How do I use them? See Hook (2016), page 46.

Relevant tasks: Describe, explain, discuss. What is it like? What do you notice? Why do you think it is like that? What does it make you wonder?

This map deliberately prompts for deeper thinking for each characteristic in the HOT SOLO Describe map and rubric. Sometimes called "the one map to rule them all", it asks students to describe, infer (explain) and wonder (or evaluate) each attribute. It can be constructed from separate SOLO strip maps (see above) in collaborative group work.

Change – mixing, heating and cooling. Adding heat energy to (heating) or removing it from (cooling) a material provides many opportunities to study change, as does mixing common materials.

Students use their senses to look for: change in form, colour or temperature; change in energy – production (exothermic) or loss (endothermic) of heat; change in pH (acidity or alkalinity); change in light, heat or sound emitted; formation of gases (often appearing as bubbles); formation of a precipitate (insoluble particles); or decomposition of organic matter. With younger students, food technology is often used to train them in observing and reporting on change (eg, popping corn, dissolving jelly crystals, making pancakes, freezing ice cream, melting chocolate, heating jellybeans).

Students can self-assess their ability to observe these changes using a SOLO rubric (Exhibit 2.20).

Exhibit 2.20: SOLO self-assessment rubric for observing, inferring about and extending ideas about change

Functioning knowledge	Prestructural	Unistructural	Multistructural	Relational	Extended abstract
Nature of science – observation Science capability – gather data	I need help to observe the event.	I can observe the event if I am told what to look for or measure.	I can observe the event (or evidence from it) but I am not sure what I am looking for.	I can observe the event (or evidence from it) and explain (infer based on) what I observe … because … so that	… and I use repeated observations to improve their reliability. I use these skills to observe scientific phenomena in everyday life. I connect my observation and inference with the big concepts in science.
Effective strategies *(add teacher and student suggestions)*				HookED SOLO Describe++ map and rubric	

It is worth thinking carefully to plan the heating, cooling and mixing activities so that they lead to both **reversible change** (physical change) and **irreversible change** (chemical change) (Exhibit 2.21). In this way, when students gather data, they can consolidate their surface understanding of change. The examples that follow show how to support this approach with a SOLO Describe++ map focused on mixing two materials (Exhibit 2.22) and a SOLO Describe++ triple strip map on changes when adding heat energy to or removing it from a solid, liquid and/or gas (Exhibit 2.23).

Exhibit 2.21: Examples of reversible and irreversible changes

Reversible change (physical change) Temporary; can be undone; no new materials formed	Irreversible change (chemical change) Permanent; cannot be undone; new materials formed
Water (liquid) to water (solid) – freezes (remove heat energy) Water (solid) to water (liquid) – melts (add heat energy)	Mixture of vinegar and bicarbonate of soda
Water (solid) to water (gas) – sublimes (add heat energy) Water (gas) to water (solid) – deposition (remove heat energy)	Mixture of cement powder, sand and water changes to concrete
Dissolving a solid in a solvent – salt in water (liquid) Add heat energy to evaporate off the water and you are left with the salt	Mixture of water plus plaster of Paris
Mixing icing sugar and chocolate sprinkles	Mixing water and cornflour (thickening)
Melting and cooling chocolate	Making bread
Changing shape	Making kimchi
Change elasticity or stretchiness of a slinky or rubber band	Rusting
Blowing up a balloon	Burning paper

Exhibit 2.22: HookED SOLO Describe++ map to describe, explain and wonder about changes when you mix two materials – vinegar and bicarbonate of soda

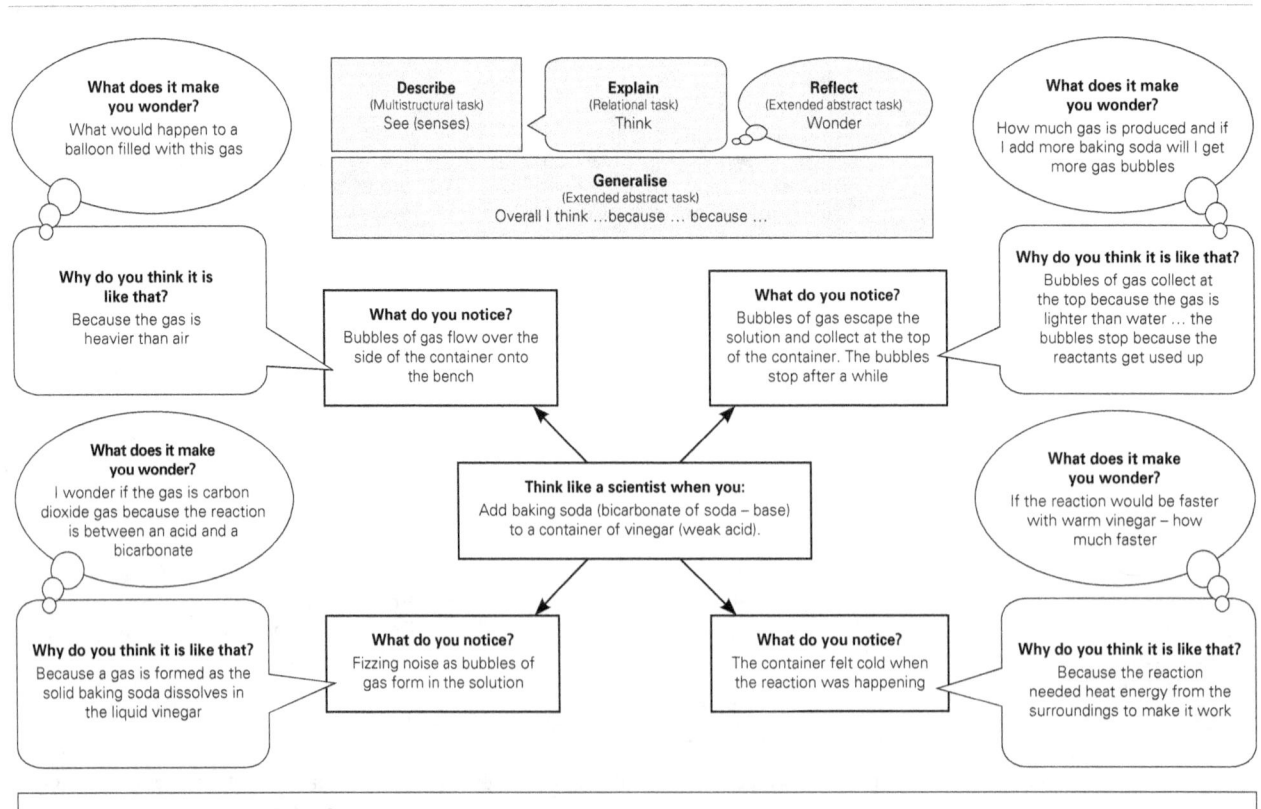

Overall what do you think it was all about?
Overall I think a chemical reaction took place – I think this because I noticed several changes. The baking soda (solid) dissolved in the vinegar (liquid) forming a new product, a gas. The temperature changed, suggesting energy was needed to help the reaction take place.

© HookED, Pam Hook, 2011. All rights reserved. Adapted from HOT SOLO Describe map with permission ©Hooked on Thinking, 2004.

Exhibit 2.23: HookED SOLO Describe++ triple strip map to describe, explain and wonder about changes when adding heat energy to or removing it from a solid, liquid and/or gas

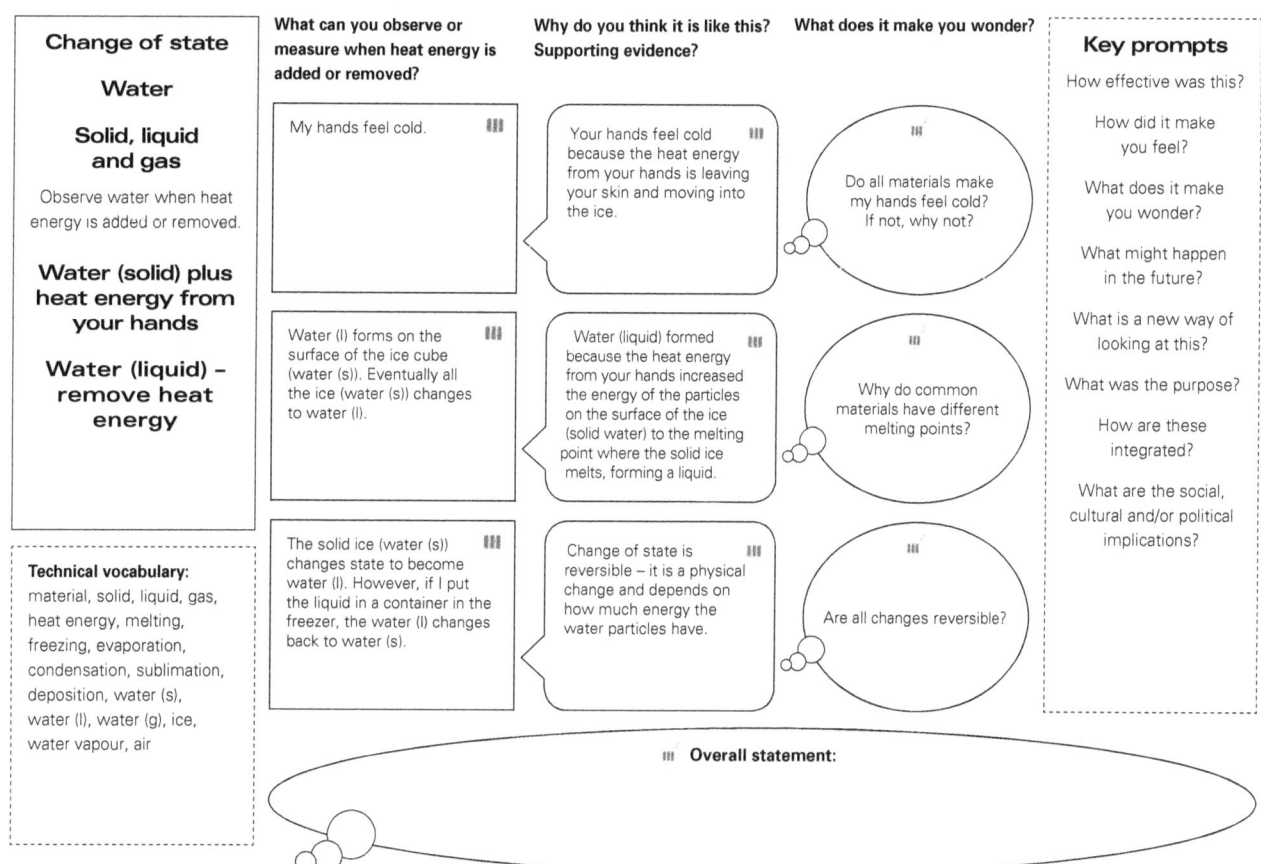

©HookED, Pam Hook, 2012. All rights reserved.

Using the HOT SOLO Sequence map and rubric

The HOT SOLO Sequence map and rubric clarify the sequence of ideas and events so they prompt deep thinking when interpreting data.

How do I use them? See Hook and Mills (2011), page 36 and the instructional video, HookED SOLO Sequence Map Animation (**https://youtu.be/-qphjxuKv40**).

Relevant tasks: Sequence. What is the order?

Physical (reversible) and chemical (irreversible) change. Physical and chemical change is easier for students to understand when they understand the nature of pure substances and mixtures (Box 2.1). This also helps them explore the extraction and processing of raw materials and their ores from the earth's crust.

Box 2.1: Pure substances and mixtures

A **pure substance** contains only one element or compound. An **impure substance** or **mixture** contains a number of different elements or compounds. Its substances are not chemically joined together. These impurities change the properties of the pure substance. For example, adding other substances (impurities) to pure water will change the boiling point of water (a property of pure water).

A mixture can be separated by **physical methods**, with the choice of method based on the mixture. For example:

- if a substance does not dissolve in a solvent, it is insoluble (eg, sawdust, sand and gravel) and we can separate the mixture using decanting and/or filtration
- if a solid substance dissolves in a solvent, it is soluble (eg, salt is soluble in water, forming a solution of salt and water) – we can separate the solid substance from the solution using evaporation and can separate the solvent from the solution using simple distillation
- if two or more liquids are mixed together, we can separate them using fractional distillation
- we can separate dissolved solids from each other using chromatography.

Sequence the steps in separating a mixture. When students explore ways of separating mixtures, they write the methods they use in a sequence of steps that others can follow. The activity is more challenging if the different mixtures allow students to use several separation methods in order to separate the materials. For example, separating a mixture of:

- sawdust, salt and sand requires dissolving, decanting, evaporating and filtering
- sawdust, salt and iron-rich black sand requires all of the above and magnetism
- different solids in a liquid requires chromatography. For example, the colour pigments in black ballpoint ink or confectionery dissolve in a solvent and travel at different speeds up the chromatography paper.

The SOLO Sequence map deepens understanding of a process. After writing the sequence of steps explaining the *how* and *why* of separating mixtures, students can use their deeper understanding to better infer about and interpret news reports on purifying a contaminated water source or clearing up an oil spill.

Exhibit 2.24 presents an example of using a SOLO Sequence map to record the steps involved in separating a mixture of salt, cork and sand. Exhibit 2.25 is an accompanying SOLO Sequence self-assessment rubric for this task.

Exhibit 2.24: HOT SOLO Sequence map for separating a mixture of salt, cork and sand

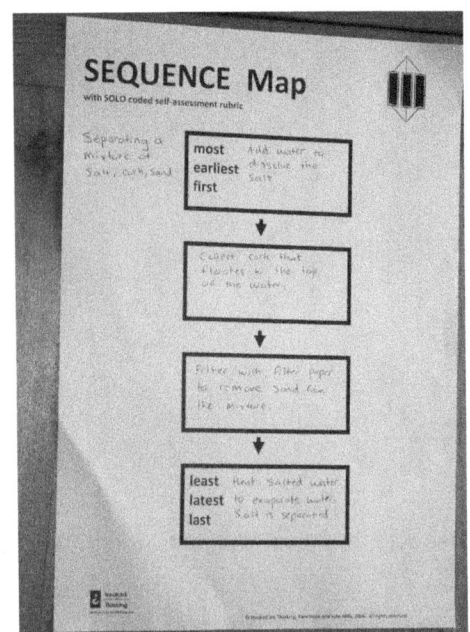

Add water to dissolve the salt

Collect cork that floats to the top of the water

Filter with filter paper to remove sand from the mixture

Heat salted water to evaporate water. Salt is separated

Exhibit 2.25: HOT SOLO Sequence self-assessment rubric for separating a mixture of salt, cork and sand

	Prestructural	Unistructural	Multistructural	Relational	Extended abstract
Sequence the steps in separating a mixture of salt, cork and sand	I need help to sequence the steps in separating a mixture of salt, cork and sand.	I can identify the place that one of the steps comes in the sequence of separating the mixture.	I can order the steps in separating the mixture …	… **and** I can explain the order …	… **and** I can look at the steps in a new way (generalise, evaluate, predict, create).
Effective strategies *(add teacher and student suggestions)*				"because"	

32

Using the HOT SOLO Classify map and rubric

The HOT SOLO Classify Map and rubric clarifies understanding by categorising or grouping ideas on the basis of similarities, shared qualities or characteristics. In this way they prompt deep thinking when interpreting data.

How do I use them? See Hook and Mills (2011), page 39 and the instructional video, HookED SOLO Classify Map Animation (**https://youtu.be/PAbyd3ToV4U**).

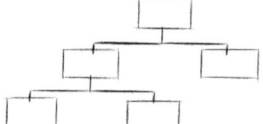

Relevant tasks: Which group or category?

Classifying requires students to make connections between ideas and in doing so they think more deeply. When scientists group or classify objects on the basis of their material composition, or common materials on the basis of their properties, they develop frameworks similar to the one in Exhibit 2.26.

Exhibit 2.26: A framework for classifying materials

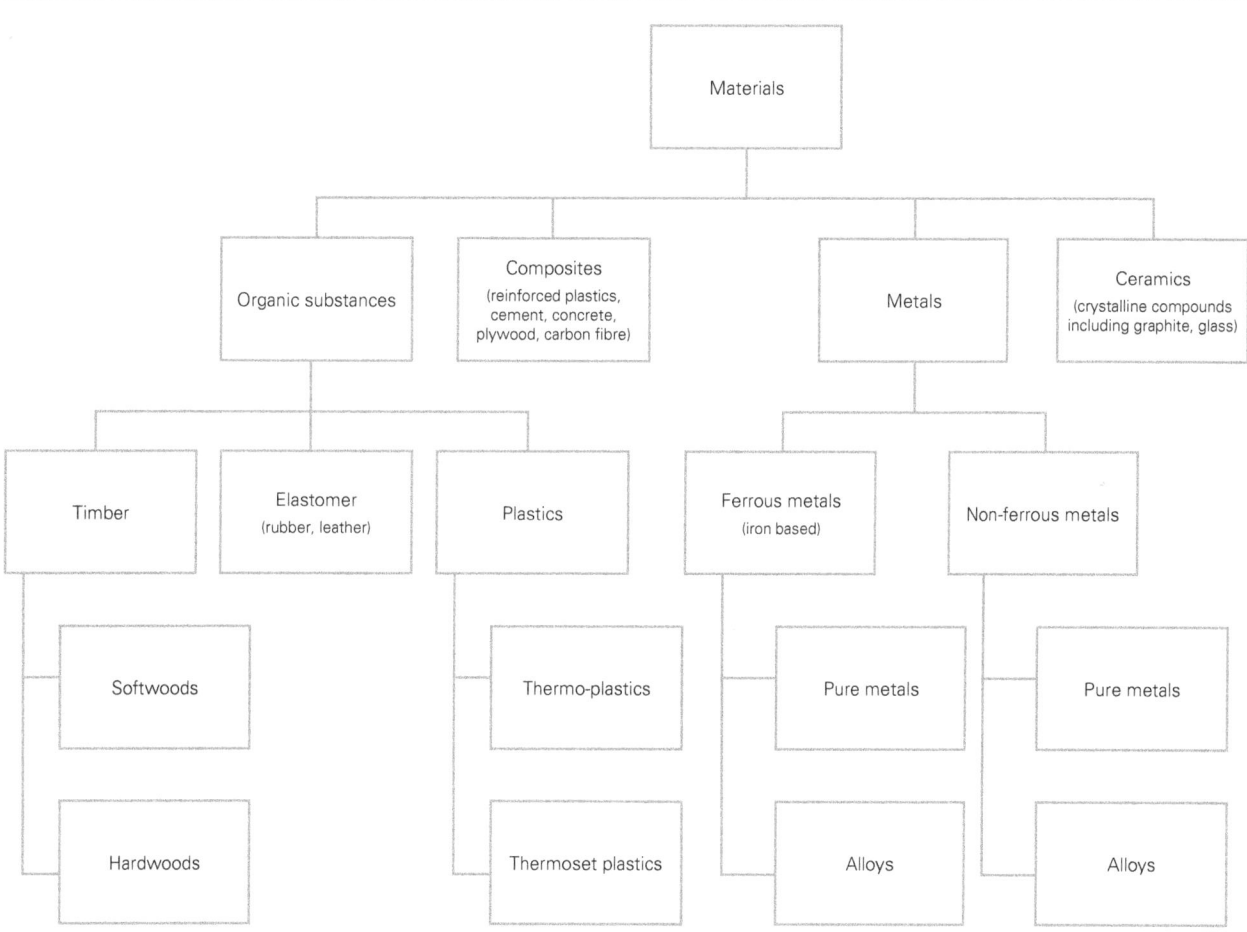

Primary, intermediate and secondary students create simpler hierarchies using predictions and then testing to classify common materials as: floaters or sinkers; plastic, metal or wood; solid, liquid or gas; shiny or dull. When students classify common materials on the basis of similarities in properties, they make connections that deepen their understanding of the material world. Their understanding also deepens when they explain the basis for their classification. Each connection enhances their ability to interpret and make inferences about what they observe.

Both the SOLO Classify map and SOLO hexagons are useful when searching for a basis on which to group common materials. Exhibit 2.27 is an example of using a SOLO Classify map to group different kinds of matter. Exhibit 2.28 is a SOLO Classify self-assessment rubric for a task of classifying materials as solids, liquids or gases.

Exhibit 2.27: HOT SOLO Classify map for grouping different kinds of matter

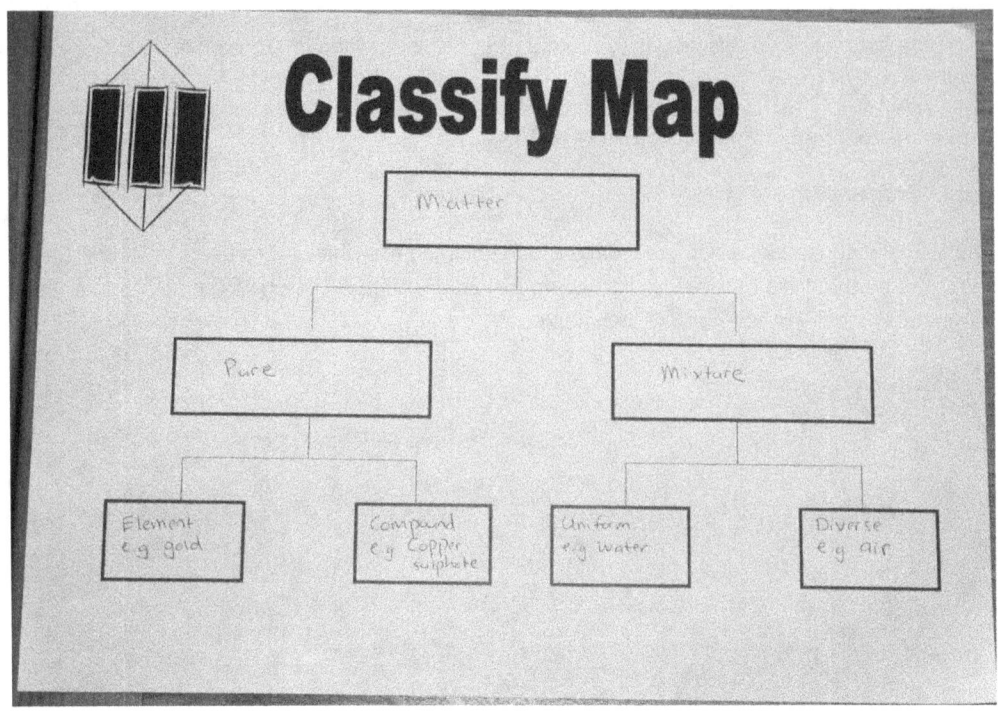

Exhibit 2.28: HOT SOLO Classify self-assessment rubric for classifying common materials as solids, liquids or gases

	Prestructural	Unistructural	Multistructural	Relational	Extended abstract
Solid, liquid or gas	I need help to classify common materials as a solid, liquid or gas.	I can classify common materials as solids.	I can classify common materials as solids, liquids or gases ...	... **and** I can explain the reasons for my classification ...	... **and** I can predict the effect of adding or removing heat energy on materials.
Effective strategies *(add teacher and student suggestions)*					

Using the HOT SOLO Compare and Contrast map and rubric

The HOT SOLO Compare and Contrast map and rubric identify similarities and differences between objects and ideas. In this way they prompt deep thinking when interpreting data.

How do I use them? See Hook and Mills (2011), page 42 and the instructional video, HookED SOLO Compare and Contrast Map Animation (https://youtu.be/KY0YaOBzlpM).

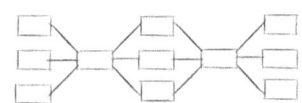

Relevant tasks

- Compare and contrast. How is it similar? How is it different? Why is it similar? Why is it different? Overall, to what extent is it similar or different?
- Which group or category?

Exhibit 2.29 shows how a student has completed a SOLO Compare and Contrast map on copper and sulphur. Students can self-assess this and other compare and contrast tasks using the SOLO Compare and Contrast rubric in Exhibit 2.30.

Exhibit 2.29: HOT SOLO Compare and Contrast map for two common materials – copper and sulphur

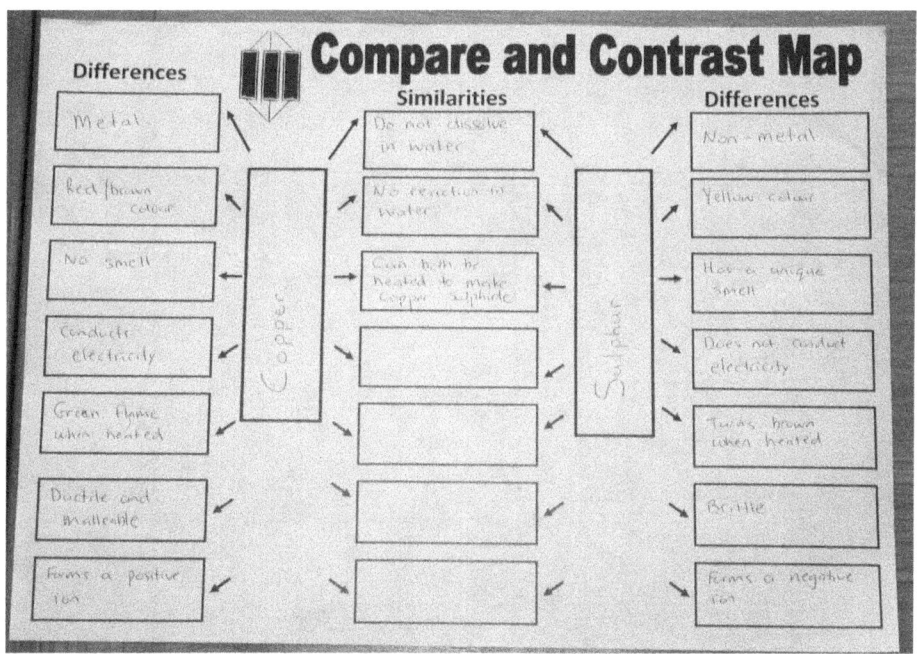

Exhibit 2.30: HOT SOLO Compare and Contrast self-assessment rubric

	Prestructural	Unistructural	Multistructural	Relational	Extended abstract
Compare and contrast a with b (How are they similar? How are they different?)	I can identify the objects and ideas associated with a and b but I need help to compare and contrast them.	I can identify one relevant similarity and one relevant difference between a and b.	I can identify several relevant similarities and differences between a and b …	… **and** give reasons for these similarities and differences …	… **and** look at the similarities and differences in a new way (generalise, evaluate, predict, create).
Effective strategies *(add teacher and student suggestions)*					

Using the HOT SOLO Analyse (part–whole) map and rubric

The HOT SOLO Analyse (part–whole) map and rubric analyse an object or idea by identifying the constituent parts and by working out the purpose and thus the importance of each part to the whole. In this way they prompt deep thinking when interpreting data.

How do I use them? See Hook and Mills (2011), page 48.

Relevant tasks: Part–whole analysis. What are the parts? How do they work together in the whole?

Exhibit 2.31 shows how a student has completed a SOLO Analyse map for a Bunsen burner. Students can self-assess this and other part–whole analyses using the SOLO Analyse rubric in Exhibit 2.32.

Exhibit 2.31: HOT SOLO Analyse map for a part–whole analysis of a Bunsen burner

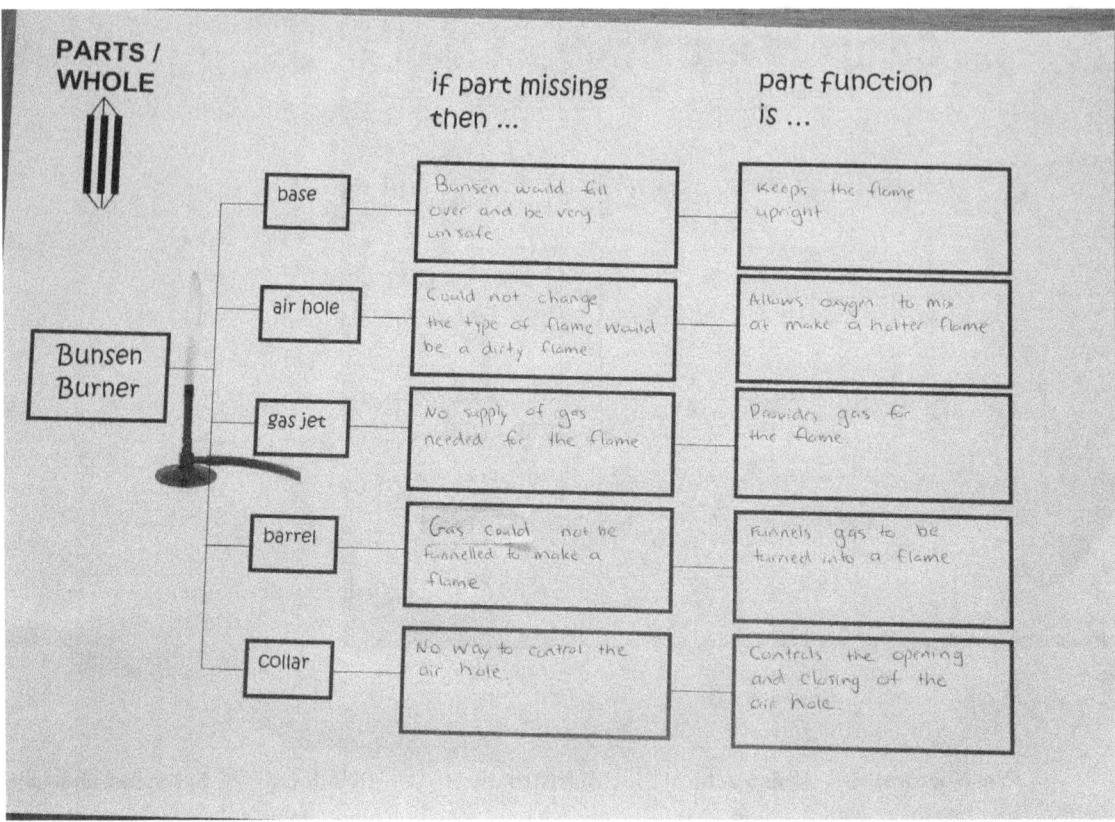

Exhibit 2.32: HOT SOLO Analyse self-assessment rubric

	Prestructural	Unistructural	Multistructural	Relational	Extended abstract
Analyse [X]. (What are the parts and how do they work?)	I can identify [X] but I need help to identify the relevant parts.	I can identify [X] and one relevant part.	I can identify [X] and several relevant parts ...	... **and** I can explain what would happen to [X] if a part was missing ...	... **and** I can generalise about the function of each part and evaluate their contribution to [X].
Effective strategies *(add teacher and student suggestions)*				"because"	"Overall I think ... because ... because ..."

Using models: the particle model

Another strategy for students to acquire and consolidate deeper understanding of the material world is to introduce the particle model as a significant next step in understanding the material world. In describing states of matter and changes in states of matter, students reach a point at which they need a richer vocabulary than *solid*, *liquid* and *gas*. Explaining, interpreting and making inferences about change – mixing and reversible and irreversible change, evaporation, melting, atoms, molecules and so on – is a struggle without referring to the particle nature of matter (Box 2.2 on page 38).

To consolidate deep understanding using the particle nature of matter students need to understand density and expand their scientific vocabulary to describe the changes and properties they observe. Many teachers use drama and role play as learning strategies. Students become moving "particles" in a container (bounded by the classroom walls, floor and ceiling) to which "heat energy" is added or removed.

Exhibit 2.33 shows how to use specific question prompts to help students to make inferences and apply their new understanding to everyday life, consolidating their deep understanding.

Exhibit 2.33: Question prompts to consolidate deep understanding of solids, liquids and gases

What can you observe, measure or notice?	Why do you think it is like this? What can you infer from what you notice?	How can you apply this understanding in everyday life?
Solid		
A solid retains a fixed volume and shape.	A solid is rigid – particles in a solid are locked into place.	Any measuring instrument like a ruler or weight
A solid is not easily compressible.	There is little free space between particles in a solid.	Blade of a spade or axe
A solid does not flow easily; it stays in one place and can be held.	A solid is rigid – particles cannot move/slide past one another.	iPad or book
Liquid		
A liquid changes shape to suit the container but it always takes up the same amount of space. Its volume remains the same.	Particles in a liquid can move/slide past one another.	Pouring a bottle of fizzy drink into paper cups
A liquid is not easily compressible.	A liquid has little free space between particles.	Water pistols, water fountains
A liquid can be poured; it flows easily and can be hard to hold.	Particles in a liquid can move/slide past one another.	Bathroom shower
Gas		
A gas spreads out and changes shape and volume to fill up the container.	Particles in a gas can move past one another.	Blowing gas (air or helium) into a balloon (container). Can smell gas particles after opening a container (eg, perfume)
A gas is compressible.	A gas has lots of free space between particles.	Compressed air in an 11-litre scuba tank. If the air was at standard pressure, the container would need to be about 2 500 litres in volume.
A gas flows easily.	Particles in a gas can move past one another.	Air flowing over an aircraft wing, vacuum cleaner, hair dryer

Box 2.2: Particle nature of matter

Each state of matter is composed of particles at different densities (number of particles per unit volume). A solid has more particles per unit of volume than in a liquid, and a liquid has more than in a gas.

We can change the density of the particles to cause a physical change of state by adding or removing heat energy.

Adding heat energy to water in its solid state (ice) changes the density of the particles (**decreases** the density of the particles) and its state changes from water as a solid to water as a liquid.

Removing heat energy from steam (gaseous water) changes the density of the particles (**increases** the density), changing it from water in a gaseous state to water in a liquid state.

The relationship between states of matter and heat energy

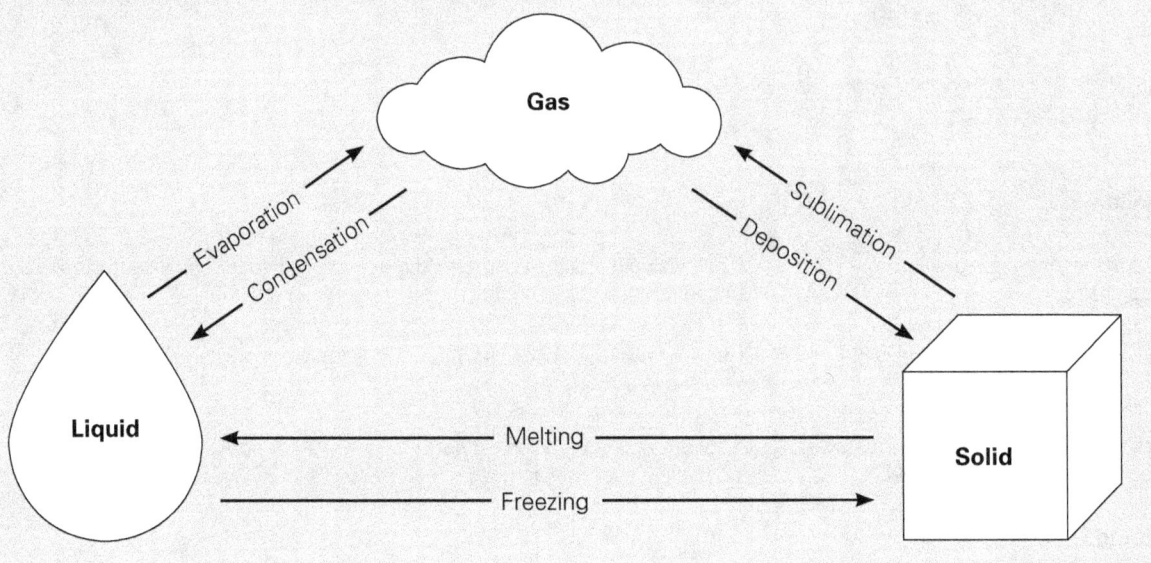

Using other strategies

Recent research by Hattie and Donoghue (2016) identifies (and ranks using effect size or ES) learning strategies for acquiring and consolidating surface information – that is, gathering and interpreting data. Note ES 0.4 is the hinge point.[3] Here we describe some of the more effective strategies for helping students acquire new science vocabulary (using mnemonics, and underlining and highlighting) and extending understanding to other contexts (far transfer and seeing patterns to new situations).

Mnemonics (above average ES 0.76). Mnemonics are useful when students are trying to acquire surface knowledge about the material world and waste management through the atomic number and location of elements (materials) in the periodic table or the reactivity series of metals.

Knowing about the elements is important for understanding waste management. It helps students understand the raw material and ores where the elements are found and the physical and chemical changes needed to extract them. Exhibit 2.34 unpacks a mnemonic for the metal reactivity series and Exhibit 2.35 for the first 20 elements of the periodic table.

Exhibit 2.34: Mnemonic for the metal reactivity series

Highly reactive to unreactive

Please **S**top **C**alling **M**e **A** **C**ute **Z**ebra **I** **L**ike **H**er **C**all **S**mart **G**oat

Potassium > **S**odium > **C**alcium > **M**agnesium > **A**luminium > (**C**arbon)* > **Z**inc > **I**ron > **L**ead > **H**ydrogen > **C**opper > **S**ilver > **G**old

---

Note: * Carbon is non-metal.

---

3   An effect size of $d = 0.2$ may be judged to have a small effect, $d = 0.4$ a medium effect and $d = 0.6$ a large effect on outcomes. The hinge point, $d = 0.4$, is an effect size at which an initiative can be said to be having a "greater than average influence" on achievement (Hattie 2012).

Exhibit 2.35: Mnemonic for the first 20 elements in the periodic table

Happy	**He**nry	**Li**ves	**Be**side	**B**orn	**C**ottage	**N**ear	**O**ur
H Hydrogen	He Helium	Li Lithium	Be Beryllium	B Boron	C Carbon	N Nitrogen	O Oxygen
Friend	**Ne**lly	**Na**ncy	**MgAl**len.		**Si**lly	**P**atrick	**S**tays
F Fluorine	Ne Neon	Na Sodium	Mg Magnesium	Al Aluminium	Si Silicon	P Phosphorus	S Sulphur
Close.	**Ar**thur	**K**isses	**Ca**rrie.				
Cl Chlorine	Ar Argon	K Potassium	Ca Calcium				

Underlining and highlighting (ES 0.50). Selective highlighting helps students attend to explicit text cues when acquiring surface information from a science text. When they use highlighting to differentiate the text by SOLO level, they learn more about the vocabulary and text patterns of scientific writing, as well as making different levels of thinking (surface, deep and conceptual) visible (Exhibit 2.36).

Exhibit 2.36: Highlighting a text to show the different SOLO levels

Diffusion

Diffusion is a process where particles travel from an area of high concentration to a lower concentration. Diffusion can occur in liquids and gases because the particles are free to move. When the particles are close together they are more likely to collide with one another. These collisions will make them move away from each other. High temperatures can speed up diffusion because the particles have more kinetic energy; this causes the particles to move faster and collide more often. Diffusion occurs in our lungs when our alveoli exchange oxygen into the bloodstream and carbon dioxide out of the blood stream. The concentration gradient of each substance allows this process to occur efficiently.

Key: Multistructural Relational Extended abstract

Far transfer (ES0.80) and seeing patterns to new situations (ES1.14). A powerful pedagogical strategy is to support students to extend and transfer their initial focus on data gathering and making inferences about common materials to the implications for waste management and bigger picture thinking. Box 2.3 lists some of the big ideas about the material world that help students understand what they are observing in the material world.

Using a HookED Describe++ map can be a useful way of prompting students to extend what they have gathered and interpreted about the material world (Exhibit 2.37). Students can then test their big picture thinking using a SOLO self-assessment rubric (Exhibit 2.38).

Box 2.3: Some BIG ideas about the material world
- Matter is made from particles (discrete fundamental units called atoms).
- Matter can't be destroyed. Objects and materials can be, but the matter must remain in another form.
- Matter contains energy.
- Matter is as old as the universe – a "new" product is never really new in terms of matter.
- Chemical and physical properties of materials can be explained by:
  - the structure and arrangement of these particles (atoms, ions and molecules)
  - the forces between them.
- Chemical reactions can only happen if the reactant particles collide with enough energy.

Exhibit 2.37: HookED SOLO Describe++ map to prompt students to gather and interpret data and conceptualise the big picture

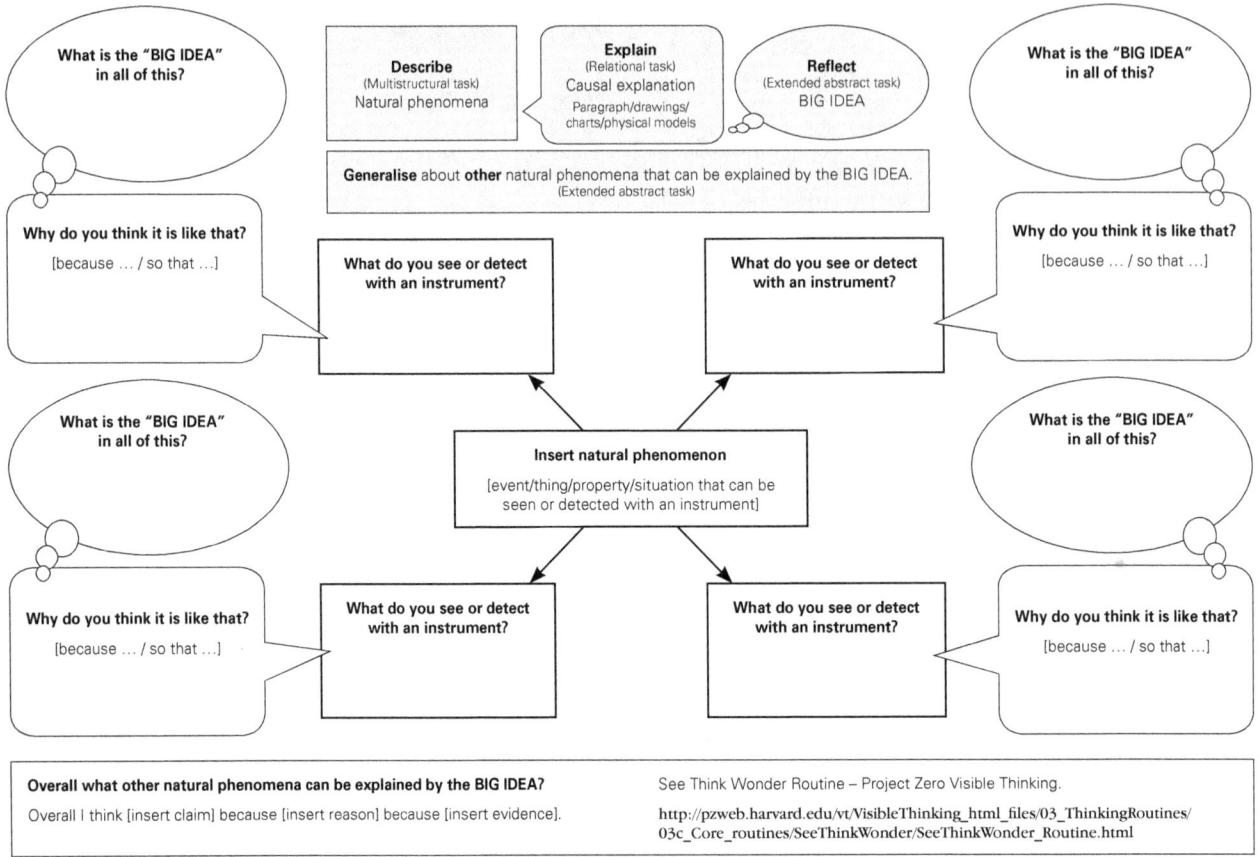

© HookED, Pam Hook, 2011. All rights reserved. Adapted from HOT SOLO Describe map with permission ©Hooked on Thinking, 2004.

Exhibit 2.38: SOLO self-assessment rubric to describe, explain and extend a scientific phenomenon

Declarative knowledge	**Prestructural**	**Unistructural**	**Multistructural**	**Relational**	**Extended abstract**
Describe, explain and extend a phenomenon (something detectable)	I need help to explain what happened.	I can describe *what* happened **but** I make no connection to any science understanding.	I can describe what happened and *how* it happened **but** the connection to science understanding is incomplete.	I can describe what happened and how. I can use my science understanding to explain *why* something happened …	… **and** I can make a generalisation about the phenomenon, referring to a science concept or the implications for an everyday application like waste management.

3. Use evidence

Learners support their ideas with evidence and look for evidence supporting others' explanations.
(Science capabilities, Ministry of Education nd)

Using evidence (relational level)

Thank you, Fat Tony. However, in the future I would prefer a nondescript briefcase to the sack with a dollar sign on it. (Mayor "Diamond" Joe Quimby, *The Simpsons*)

Using evidence is a SOLO relational-level task. It is a response to curiosity – to "why should I believe you?" It is that moment when we check the briefcase *is* full of money (a trope in many TV shows).

We see, observe, notice the nondescript briefcase or (for Mayor Quimby) the sack with a dollar sign on it – we gather data. We infer from what we observe and from our previous experience of watching these kinds of shows that the briefcase contains neatly stacked large-denomination bills. However, if we are thinking critically about the plot then we need to see evidence that the briefcase does contain money. We need evidence before we accept the observation and inference.

You can make a claim about a scientific phenomenon and support the claim with reasons but until you can front with evidence to support your reasons, your claim is unlikely to attract much support. Similarly, when you listen to the claims others make, if you are thinking like a scientist you will delay acceptance until you have evidence supporting their explanations.

"Use evidence" questions

We think like a scientist when we ask ourselves and others, "So where is the evidence? Why should I believe you? Why should they believe my results? How do you know that?" In the material world, evidence might be qualitative or quantitative:

- We might ask for **qualitative evidence** of the observed change when a common material is mixed, heated or cooled – for example, evidence to support the observation that adding heat energy to surfboard wax caused the wax to change state and melt or that repeatedly shaking a bottle of tomato sauce allowed the sauce to flow more easily.
- We might ask for **quantitative evidence** of a change in pH of a solution, change in volume (cm^3) of gas released, change in temperature (°C) or change in mass (g). You may wish to measure the electrical conductivity of different metal wires of the same cross-sectional area and length using a multimeter or simply observe how metals react in air, cold water, warm water and weak acids.

This qualitative and quantitative evidence may take the form of data recorded in a results table, log-book, digital recordings, images or video. It may be shown with data from duplicated or replicated trials by the same or different groups. The evidence may show the observations and measurements organised or represented in different ways – in averages, pie charts or bar charts.

Exhibit 3.1: Using evidence in summary

To **use evidence** (a SOLO relational-level task) is to make connections between what is observed and evidence. It is to support explanations or interpretations by making links to evidence that supports them.	Example: Look for evidence to support the inference that water and air are needed for iron nails to rust. Test iron nails stored under the following conditions: 1. Iron nail + water + air in sealed test tube 2. Iron nail + water (no air) in sealed test tube 3. Iron nail + air (no water): use calcium chloride to absorb any water) in sealed test tube.

Progress when thinking with the "use evidence" capability

When we think with the capability "use evidence", we ask:

- What do I know about using evidence? What is it? *Declarative knowledge*
- How well do I know how to use evidence (directed, supported, independent use)? *Functioning knowledge – skill*
- How likely am I to use evidence? *Attitude – will*
- How frequently (how often) do I use evidence? *Behaviour*
- How flexibly (in different contexts, with different methods) do I use evidence? *Behaviour*

Students can show progress in any or all of the above. Thinking like a scientist about truth is tricky. Any claim made about a phenomenon in the material world must be testable, tested and re-tested. It must be both reliable and valid (Box 3.1). To think like a scientist is to be open to changing your mind – to be open to being wrong. In science you can never prove a scientific truth; you can only disprove it. So a claim is true only up to the time when new evidence shows it is not true. As the examples that follow show, SOLO maps highlight the increasing cognitive complexity of these questions:

- What do you know? Make a claim …
- Where is your evidence? Why does your evidence support the claim?

When students explore the material world and the wicked problems of waste management, the evidence comes from their data. When they claim that solids and liquids have mass and take up space, they provide evidence (data) to support both of these claims. Thinking about gas is more challenging. What evidence (data) could they provide that proves gas has mass and takes up space – that gas is matter? One approach is to use a carbonated drink maker to show how gas in a cylinder can be introduced to a syrupy solution to create a gas-liquid mixture (fizzy drink).

Box 3.1: Reliability and validity

Reliability is a measure of the consistency or repeatability of an observation or measurement. We can use the repeatability of a result as evidence for a claim. To be reliable the experimental measurement or observation must be able to be repeated with similar results or another tester must be able to repeat the observation or experiment with similar results.

Validity checks on the truthiness of the overall experiment. It checks the use of random sample groups, controls and experimental design, and whether anything in the way the experiment has been conducted would let the results be explained in another way.

Even when the experimental results seem both reliable and valid, there is always the possibility that some other factor is responsible.

Note: Section 4 deals with measures of reliability and validity in more detail.

Strategies for using evidence

In this section we present examples of learning strategies (including SOLO maps and rubrics) to prompt deep thinking when using evidence to support a claim about the material world and waste management.

Using the HOT SOLO Generalise map and rubric

The HOT SOLO Generalise map and rubric are used to back up the reliability and validity of a claim.

How do I use them? See Hook and Mills (2011), page 54 and the instructional video, HookED SOLO Generalise Map Animation (**https://youtu.be/vAiSITAgt-M**).

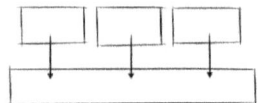

Relevant tasks: Generalise. Overall what do you think? I think … because [insert reason] … because [insert evidence].

Exhibit 3.2 shows how a SOLO Generalise map supports students in using evidence in relation to data on gas, while Exhibit 3.3 presents a completed map generalising about data on the reactivity of metals. Exhibit 3.4 is a SOLO Generalise rubric for students to self-assess how they explain scientific phenomena using evidence.

Exhibit 3.2: HOT SOLO Generalise map for using evidence when gathering and interpreting data about gas

HookED SOLO Generalise map

Generalisation
Make a claim

Gas is matter.

Explain
Support generalisation with explanation
(measure of reliability)

Because gas takes up space and has mass. Every time I fill a netball with compressed air (gas), the netball increases in mass and space. The mass of the can of compressed air reduces in mass.

Example
Support explanation with evidence and/or examples
(measure of validity)

I am careful to use the same equipment each time. I repeat my measurements several times to make sure they are reliable, accurate and valid. I ask other students to repeat the experiment and check their results.

Evaluate generalisation –
Accept/reject/uncertain – Put to a class vote

25 out of 27 students in the class accept the claim that gas is matter.

© HookED, Pam Hook, 2015. All rights reserved. Adapted with permission from HOT SOLO Generalise map ©Hooked-on-Thinking, 2004.

Exhibit 3.3: HOT SOLO Generalise map for using evidence when gathering and interpreting data about the reactivity of metals

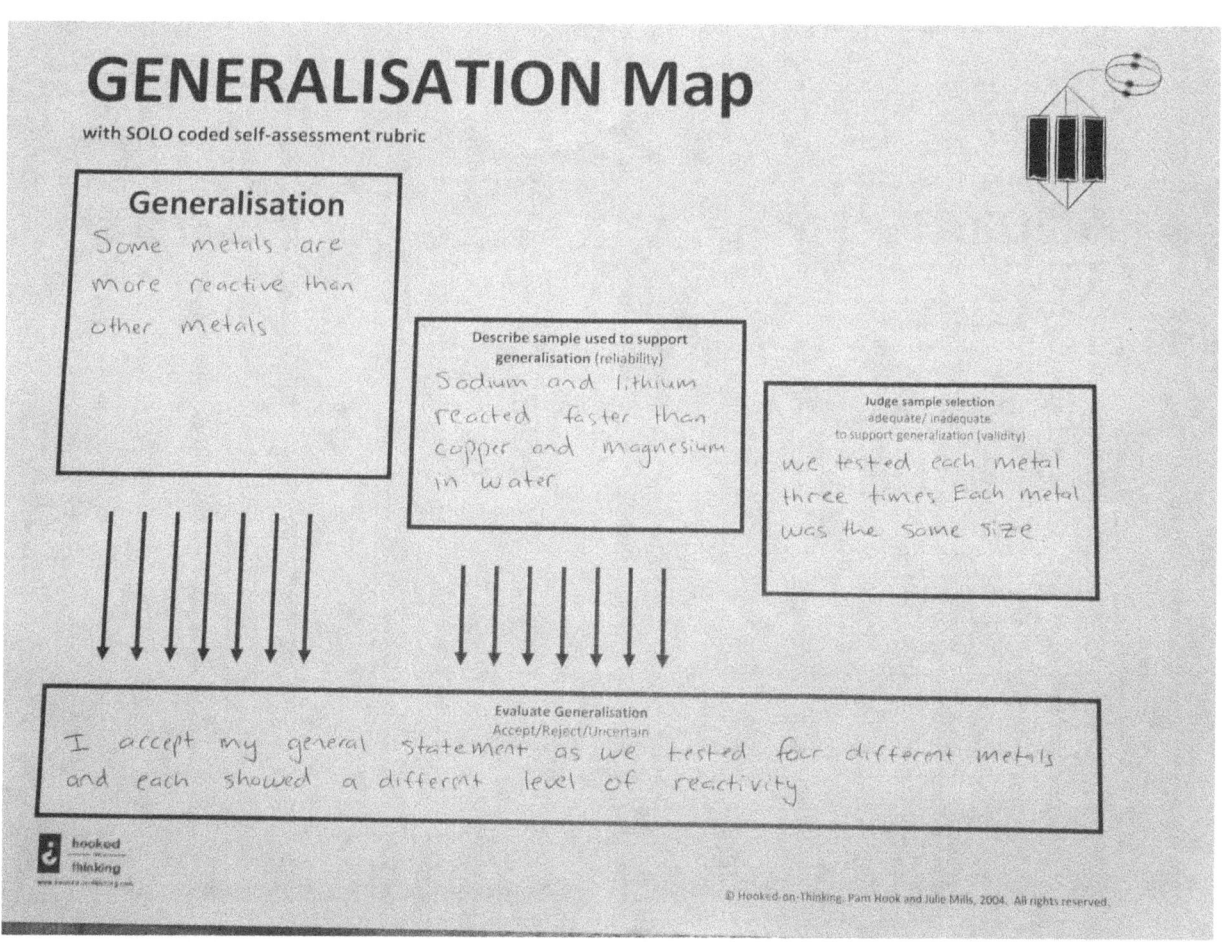

Exhibit 3.4: HOT SOLO Generalise self-assessment rubric for explaining scientific phenomena using evidence

Functioning knowledge	**Prestructural**	**Unistructural**	**Multistructural**	**Relational**	**Extended abstract**
Describe phenomenon; explain how and why it happened by connecting to science understanding; generalise by referring to evidence from a science concept.	I need help to describe [a scientific phenomenon].	I can describe [a scientific phenomenon] if I copy someone else.	I can describe [a scientific phenomenon] but I am not sure if I have the science correct.	I can describe [a scientific phenomenon] and explain *why* by making connections to science understanding …	… **and** I can extend my explanation to refer to evidence from big science ideas or concepts.

Using the HOT SOLO Predict map and rubric

The HOT SOLO Predict Map and self-assessment rubric are used to evaluate possible outcomes before selecting one as a prediction that is likely to be realised.

How do I use them? See Hook and Mills (2011), page 57 and the instructional video, HookED SOLO Predict Map Animation (**https://youtu.be/jLqyg_ACDiE**).

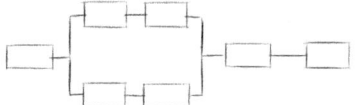

Relevant tasks: Predict. What happens next?

Exhibit 3.5 shows how a student has completed a HOT SOLO Predict map to weigh up the evidence on a prediction about factors affecting reaction rate. Exhibit 3.6 is a HOT SOLO Predict rubric students can use to self-assess their use of evidence to support and/or counter any prediction.

Exhibit 3.5: HOT SOLO Predict map for using evidence to support and/or counter a prediction about factors affecting reaction rate

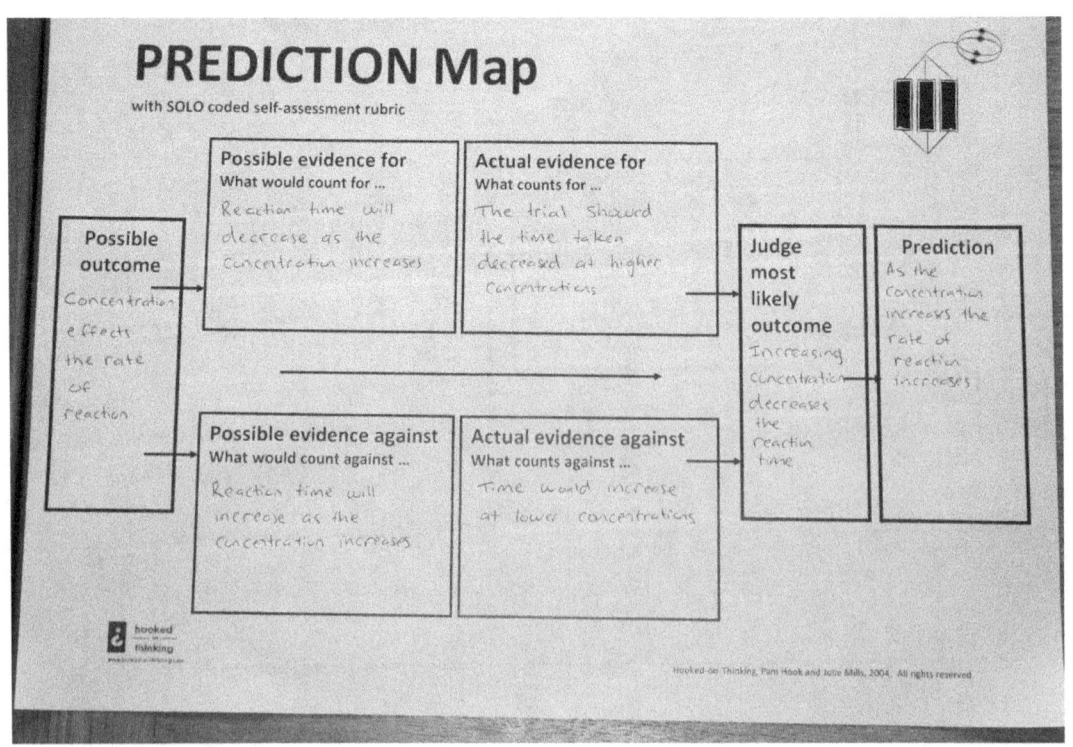

Exhibit 3.6: HOT SOLO Predict self-assessment rubric for using evidence to support and/or counter a prediction

Declarative knowledge	**Prestructural**	**Unistructural**	**Multistructural**	**Relational**	**Extended abstract**
Using evidence to support or counter (test) a prediction	I need help to use evidence to support or counter a prediction.	I report only one form of evidence, eg, supporting the prediction.	I report multiple forms of evidence, eg, supporting and countering the prediction.	I compare the multiple forms of evidence and/or counterevidence.	I evaluate the reliability and validity of the evidence and use the most likely to make a prediction.
Effective strategies *(add teacher and student suggestions)*					

Using peer-reviewed experiments that support your results

It is still important to find other results that support (or reject) a claim even if students have collected accurate and reliable data. The more data that they can find showing similar results, the more conclusive the results are likely to be.

Finding similar outcomes in other research gives the claim more credibility. However, if students find that their results differ from those of others, how do they decide if their data are more accurate and the other results have misinterpreted something?

Different results and outliers in student results provide an opportunity to discuss thinking like a scientist. Facing similar problems, scientists must continue to refine and retest their results to make them more conclusive. Both students in the classroom and scientists in a research laboratory may need to convince others to revisit and re-evaluate their own results.

In a classroom this may be as easy as comparing averaged results for a similar experiment across each group in the class. Students could discuss any similarities or differences seen in the data. However, once students are off working independently and gathering their own data, this process may be more difficult. Most of the time students should be able to find results similar to their own. Students will need to use their critical thinking to evaluate if any secondary data collected are from a reliable and accurate source. They often require strong guidance during this process. A SOLO self-assessment rubric is one support available (Exhibit 3.7).

Exhibit 3.7: SOLO self-assessment rubric for evaluating secondary data as evidence

Declarative knowledge	**Prestructural**	**Unistructural**	**Multistructural**	**Relational**	**Extended abstract**
Describe the trend in the data; explain how secondary data compare with my data; generalise by referring to both my data and secondary data	I need help to [describe the trend in the data].	I can [describe the trend in the data] if I copy someone else.	I can [describe the trend in the data] but I am not sure if I have the science correct.	I can [describe the trend in the data] and explain why these data compare with my collected data ...	... **and** I can extend my explanation to include both my data and the secondary data.

4. Critique evidence

Learners appreciate that not all questions can be answered by science.
(Science capabilities, Ministry of Education nd)

Critiquing evidence (extended abstract level)

When you think like a scientist, you look carefully at the research methods involved in collecting the evidence, the control of variables, and the statistical rigour of the results. You ask about the trustworthiness of every claim. Where is the evidence? Has anyone else replicated the research? What have you assumed in designing the experiment?

Critiquing evidence is an extended abstract task. It involves being curious about the "truthiness" of the evidence – about how any observations and measurements are interpreted and evaluated and about any evidence claimed. We not only ask about reliability and validity of the observations and measurements but also critique the experimental design or method. We actively seek counter-examples that might disprove our claim as well – asking, what is an alternative explanation; can we discount it? Students who become skilled at critiquing evidence can also design robust experiments.

"Critique evidence" questions

The really curious are never completely persuaded by "the evidence". They want to know how the evidence was obtained – how reliable it is – and whether you would get the same result if you repeated the experiment. They ask about the measuring equipment and any opportunities for measuring or instrument error. They want to know how you controlled any other variables that might influence the result. They ask if you have any other peer-reviewed papers that support what you have found. (See Exhibit 4.1 for a range of questions scientists ask in critiquing the evidence.)

Questions about controlling the variables can be especially difficult for students to answer. Perhaps the most difficult task when designing an experiment is accurately measuring the dependent variable. We must consider and control all possible factors that might influence the dependent variable; otherwise we risk collecting unfair and inconsistent data.

Exhibit 4.1: "Critique evidence" questions

- Can you think of a situation where these results may not occur?
- What did you measure and how?
- What were your independent and dependent variables? Are they all described?
- What was your control?
- Why did you choose to use that amount, set-up etc?
- How did you gather the data?
- How did you record your data?
- Was there any room for error in your data gathering or recording method?
- How did you calculate your results?
- How did you check your calculations?
- Might any other variables affect your results?
- How could you check your results?
- How consistent were your results? How can you explain any variability?
- Did any of your results surprise you? Why?
- Did you repeat the experiment? How?
- Has anyone else replicated the results?
- If you did this experiment again, what would you change?

Exhibit 4.2: Critiquing evidence in summary

To **critique evidence** (an extended abstract task) is to explore measures of data reliability and validity.	Example: Critique the data reliability and validity of the biodegradable spoons experiment (Box 4.1).

Progress when thinking with the "critiquing evidence" capability

When we think with the capability "critique evidence", we ask:

- What do I know about critiquing evidence? What is it? What is it like? *Declarative knowledge*
- How well do I know how to critique evidence (directed, supported, independent use)? *Functioning knowledge – skill*

- How likely am I to critique evidence? *Attitude – will*
- How frequently (how often) do I critique evidence? *Behaviour*
- How flexibly (in different contexts, with different methods) do I critique evidence? *Behaviour*

Students can show progress in any or all of the above. However, any critique of the evidence cannot prove that the results are "true" – at best, it can lend support to (or help reject) a hypothesis. It may do neither.

That does not mean that in science, anything goes. Scientists strive to collect the most reliable and valid data they can. They are always thinking about the quality of the evidence. They keep an open mind and are always open to revising a conclusion if better evidence comes to light.

Reliability and validity

Critiquing evidence involves considering the reliability and validity of the observed or measured data (Exhibit 4.3).

Exhibit 4.3: Questions to establish reliability and validity

Reliability	Validity
<ul><li>Are the data based on repeatable methods?</li><li>Have I repeated the experiment and found similar results?</li><li>Do multiple trials achieve the same results?</li><li>Can others perform the same experiment under the same conditions and get the same results?</li><li>Are the data consistent with other reputable sources? Have others found similar results?</li></ul>	<ul><li>Does my experimental design test my hypothesis – for example, that changes in X will affect Y? Have all the variables except the one being tested been identified and controlled?</li><li>Are all sources of error controlled?</li><li>Have all data been accurately measured, recorded and displayed?</li><li>Are my conclusions based on the data?</li></ul>

Reliability is a measure of the consistency or repeatability of the results. To establish that our results are reliable, we must be able to repeat the experiment under similar conditions and get the same or similar results (Exhibit 4.4). The variability in the results helps determine how many times we need to repeat an experiment. As general rule, the more variable your results are, the more you need to repeat the experiment. Repeating the experiment is a way of increasing the sample size. School-based experiments are usually repeated three to five times to improve their reliability.

Results also become more reliable when someone else replicates the experiment and gets the same results.

Exhibit 4.4: SOLO self-assessment rubric for using reliable evidence to support a claim

Functioning knowledge	**Prestructural**	**Unistructural**	**Multistructural**	**Relational**	**Extended abstract**
Repeated controlled experiments Multiple forms/ sources of evidence	I need help to use [evidence].	I can support a claim with [evidence] if I copy an example.	I can support a claim with [evidence] but I sometimes make mistakes and do not know how to fix them.	I can support a claim with [reliability evidence] and explain why.	I compare multiple forms of evidence and/or counter-evidence. I evaluate its reliability (and validity).
Effective strategies *(add teacher and student suggestions)*					

However, reliability is necessary but not sufficient when thinking like a scientist. A measure may be highly reliable but not valid. For example, if a measuring instrument is faulty (or if we use a flawed measuring technique), then we will repeatedly record a similar result (highly reliable) but that result will be neither accurate nor valid.

Similarly, if the experimental design is flawed – for example, the scientists have not controlled the variables, considered some key variables and/or trialled a method – then the evidence is not sufficiently reliable. For example, if a student notices that iron nails left outside for a week show signs of rusting but the nails stored in the toolbox in the dark are still shiny with no signs of rust, they might claim that nails rust (react with the air) when they are exposed to sunlight. The claim can appear to be corroborated (relational-level thinking) by the observation that rusting tools hang in an old shed – and indeed the experiment is easy for others to repeat using readily available equipment and methods.

To test the claim, you can ask other students to observe what happens if they leave 15 new nails outside in full sunlight and 15 nails from the same bag in the dark. If they repeat this experiment several times, do they get a similar result – that the nails left outside show signs of rust while the nails in the dark remain shiny? The evidence for the claim seems reliable.

The students could go further to create a model or analogy for the particles in metallic iron with annotations to represent the claim that energy from the sun triggers some kind of reaction with oxygen in the air leading a new product, iron oxide (rust), to form. An entrepreneurial student might plan a technological innovation as a barrier to shelter nails from the sun's rays – the iron nail equivalent of sunscreen – and show prototypes at a local inventors' forum.

However, all this activity is without value from a scientific perspective. The evidence is flawed because the experimental design is flawed. Regardless of the reliability and your level of confidence in your observations, when you fail to control all the variables it is easy to confuse correlation with causation.

When we look at the "truthiness" of observations and inference, we need an extra measure of "evidence" over reliability.

Challenging evidence that seems reliable

To critique the evidence, students need to cultivate a mindset that asks, "Where is the exception?" For example, if the experimental analysis suggests iron nails require light to rust, then the question is: "Can you think of an example where iron nails rust in the dark?" We need to think about confounding variables, how we could disprove this result or how we could show this hypothesis is not always true.

For the rusty nail example above, many counter-examples seem to challenge the initial results. One is that simply controlling moisture content will reveal that nails rust in the light and the dark. The evidence no longer supports the claim. In this experiment, a failure to control all the relevant variables produces a result that appears reliable but is not valid. We controlled the variables of light and dark but not moisture or wetness in the environment. If both samples of nails had been kept in moist conditions, we may have found no difference in rust levels. This example shows that evidence and even repeated experiments that result in reliable evidence are necessary but not sufficient when thinking like a scientist. To make meaning about the material world, we need reliable and valid evidence.

Validity is a measure of the accuracy or "truthiness" of the result. It asks, "Does the result measure what it is supposed to measure?" To get valid evidence, we must carefully control other variables that might influence the result and carefully check for sources of error in measuring the dependent variable, which may be caused by the measuring apparatus (instrumentation) or by humans when recording.

To get valid results, we should:

- randomise the sample groups
- follow a consistent experimental process
- control all factors that might influence the outcome of the experiment (controlled variables) apart from those being tested (independent and dependent variables)
- where relevant, include a control – keeping all conditions the same except for the one being investigated
- complement or build on other similar experiments from peers.

In addition, critiquing evidence might involve checking up on any of the following types of error:

- **Human error:** Did the researcher make mistakes when reading a scale, writing down readings or calculating the average? Did they fail to look squarely on at the scale and introduce parallax error, or inconsistently read the volume of a liquid by looking from the bottom of the meniscus? Can you ask to see the original data and rework the data?
- **Equipment limitations:** How accurate is the measuring instrument? Was the meter or scale calibrated before use? Is the instrument scale appropriate for the measurement range?
- **Observation errors:** Does the researcher know how to estimate the position of a pointer on a scale? Is the process of taking measurements interfering with the experiment?
- **Ill-defined measurement values:** Researchers may vary in their understanding of measures like "a change in colour" when adding drops of one liquid to another. Do they all agree on what constitutes "a drop" and "colour change"?
- **Inconsistent techniques and procedures:** Was the researcher careful or sloppy when replicating the experiment?

Box 4.1: Being curious about cornstarch (or potato starch) spoons

Thinking with the science capability "critique evidence" puts you in a stronger position to design reliable and valid experimental procedures.

Micro-organisms (bacteria and fungi) living in the soil, ocean and human bodies biodegrade (break down) common materials to produce energy, carbon dioxide gas and water. Some common materials biodegrade rapidly over a few weeks; others take centuries to break down.

Variables affecting biodegradation include light, water, oxygen and temperature. Biodegradation can create problems in landfills where large quantities of waste materials are actively decomposing. Relying on landfill to get rid of waste materials is not a good waste management solution because the uncontrolled biodegradation can produce dangerous levels of methane gas, groundwater pollution and unstable subsoil conditions. Managed landfills work hard to reduce biodegradation activity by keeping the site dry and airtight.

A better solution is to find ways to reduce, reuse and recycle common materials before they are discarded as waste in landfills. Any remaining common materials can be composted in an environmentally friendly, sustainable three-step process.

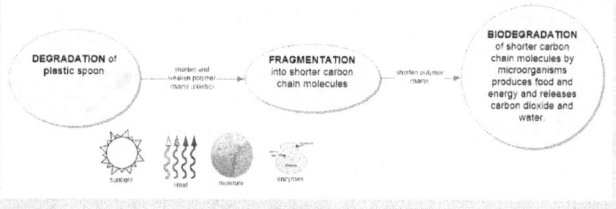

One way to reduce waste in landfills is to use more rapidly biodegraded common materials in manufacturing products. This is why common materials such as paper, cardboard and plastics are often used to make disposable cutlery. Recently manufacturers looking for a more environmentally sustainable product have developed biodegradable or compostable cutlery and plates using cornstarch (corn and sugarcane).

Students made curious by some of the more extreme claims about these cornstarch products might decide to investigate any differences in the decomposition rate of cornstarch, plastic and cardboard spoons. If they think with the capability "critique evidence", then they might sketch a draft experimental design looking like the one below.

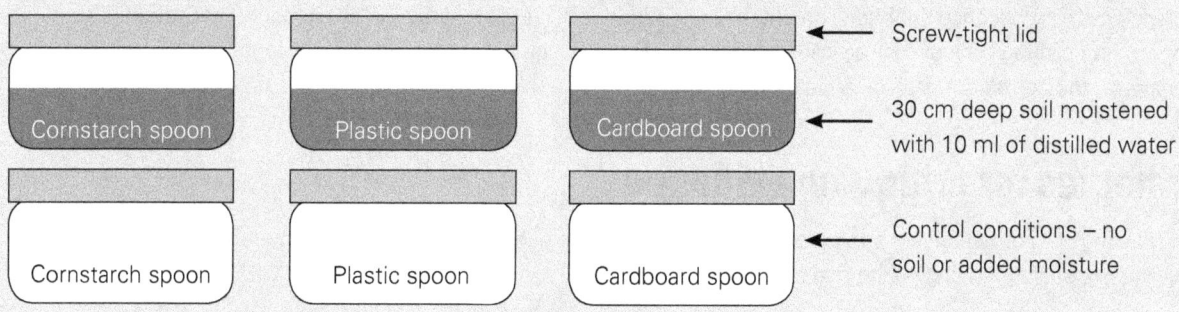

Students must first decide on:

- the variable they are going to change (**independent variable**) – here, the material used in disposable cutlery (cornstarch spoon, plastic spoon and cardboard spoon)
- the variable they are going to measure (**dependent variable**) – rate of decomposition after 30 days (eg, change in visual appearance, level of carbon dioxide accumulation and/or mass (g) of the spoons over a 30-day period).

Next they think about any other variables that might affect the decomposition rate of the spoon and how they might control them so that they do not influence the results (**key controlled variables**). Students find it hard to identify that some variables are more important to control than others and often try to control variables that are unlikely to have any great effect on the experiment (eg, same time of day, air temperature or wind velocity).

continued ...

> **Box 4.1: Being curious about cornstarch (or potato starch) spoons (continued)**
>
> One way to help students think about controlling variables is to give them time to trial the experiment several times. During this time they make mistakes and fix and modify processes that introduce errors. They more clearly understand the variables that need controlling. In this experiment, the **controlled variables** are all the other variables that might affect the decomposition rate of the cutlery, such as mass of spoon (g), surface area of spoon, mass of soil (g), type of soil, microbial activity in soil samples, temperature of soil samples, water content (moisture level) of soil samples, available air, shape of containers and amount of sunlight.
>
> Finally students think about the nature of any **experimental controls**, such as repeating the experiment in the absence of any soil micro-organisms to determine if the disposable cutlery breaks down in sunlight in this condition (photo degradation).
>
> Once they have clarified these ideas, students elaborate on their method as they plan to repeat the experiment several times to check their results are **reliable**.

Fairness, completeness and relevance

To think critically about scientific data that we or others collect and interpret, we must think beyond clarity, accuracy, validity and reliability. That is, we must routinely check for fairness, completeness and relevance – to think critically about unwarranted assumptions and prejudices, correlation and causality. We need to ask:

- Do we need to look at this from another perspective? Is there another point of view?
- Am I being fair?
- Does accepting these results advance the interests of the group reporting it?
- What am I assuming? Are my assumptions supported by the evidence?
- Is the researcher who is reporting this result made uncomfortable by having it challenged?
- To what extent is this result consistent with other scientific research?
- Is this complete? What is missing from this research?

Even when an experimental result can be shown to be reliable and valid (well controlled), unwarranted assumptions might make us look at a relationship based on correlation rather than causality. For example, we may observe an apparent causal link between Year 9 students taking an active role in an extra-curricular school recycling programme and their level of engagement in science learning in class. However, this correlation may not represent causation; it may result from another unrelated variable.

Perhaps students volunteer for the recycling programme because it often finishes a little early and they can catch the early buses. The students who travel by bus come from rural areas where they have greater lived experience of the natural and physical worlds that feature in the science programme for this term. They are initially more engaged in science learning because they have greater prior knowledge. There is correlation but no direct causation. If we changed the finishing time of the recycling programme and thus the proportion of rural students attending the recycling programme, the correlation may disappear.

Strategies for critiquing evidence

The following are some learning strategies (including SOLO maps and rubrics) to support students critiquing evidence about the material world and waste management.

Using HookED SOLO Observe Infer Evaluate map

The HookED SOLO Observe Infer Evaluate map is a modification of the HookED SOLO Describe++ map to support students when they think critically about evidence.

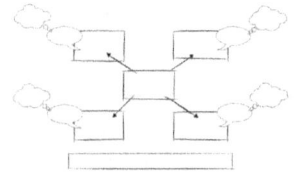

How do I use it? See Hook (2016), page 46.

Relevant tasks: What do I think? Overall I think ... because [insert inference] ... because [insert evidence to evaluate reliability and validity].

Exhibit 4.5 is an example of how students can use the SOLO Observe Infer Evaluate map to critique evidence about marshmallows expanding in a microwave.

Exhibit 4.5: HookED SOLO Observe Infer Evaluate map for critiquing evidence for gas expansion in marshmallows

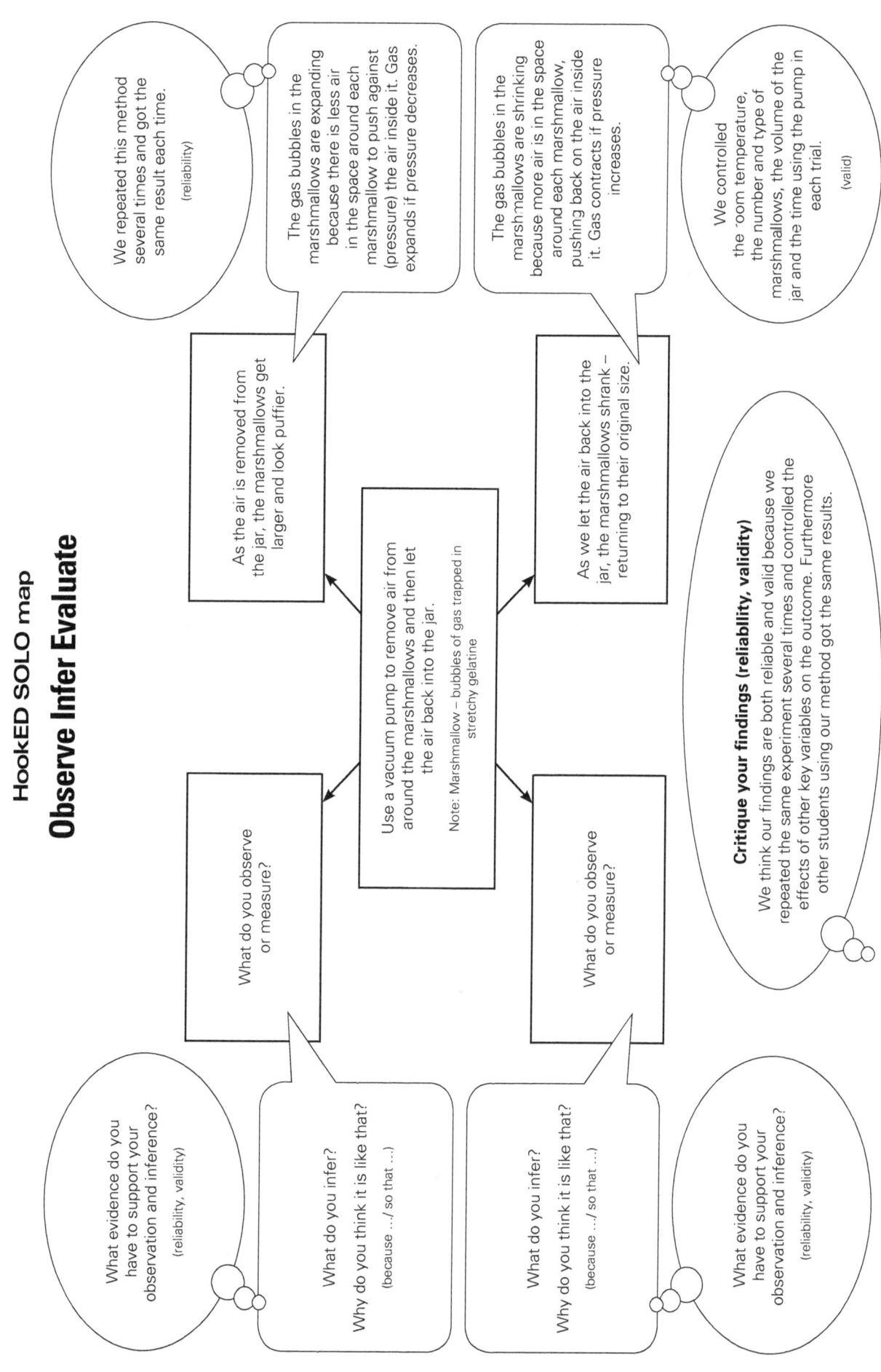

Using HOT SOLO Evaluate map and rubric

The HOT SOLO Evaluate map and rubric offer another strategy for critiquing evidence.

How do I use them? See Hook and Mills (2011), page 60.

Relevant tasks: Evaluate. What is valid?

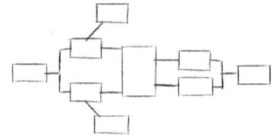

Exhibit 4.6 presents an adapted version of the HOT SOLO Evaluate map that can be used to evaluate evidence, for example, in a stretchy rubber band experiment. With the SOLO Evaluate rubrics that follow, students can self-assess their evaluation of evidence in terms of both declarative (Exhibit 4.7) and functioning (Exhibit 4.8) knowledge.

Exhibit 4.6: HookED SOLO Evaluate map for evaluating evidence

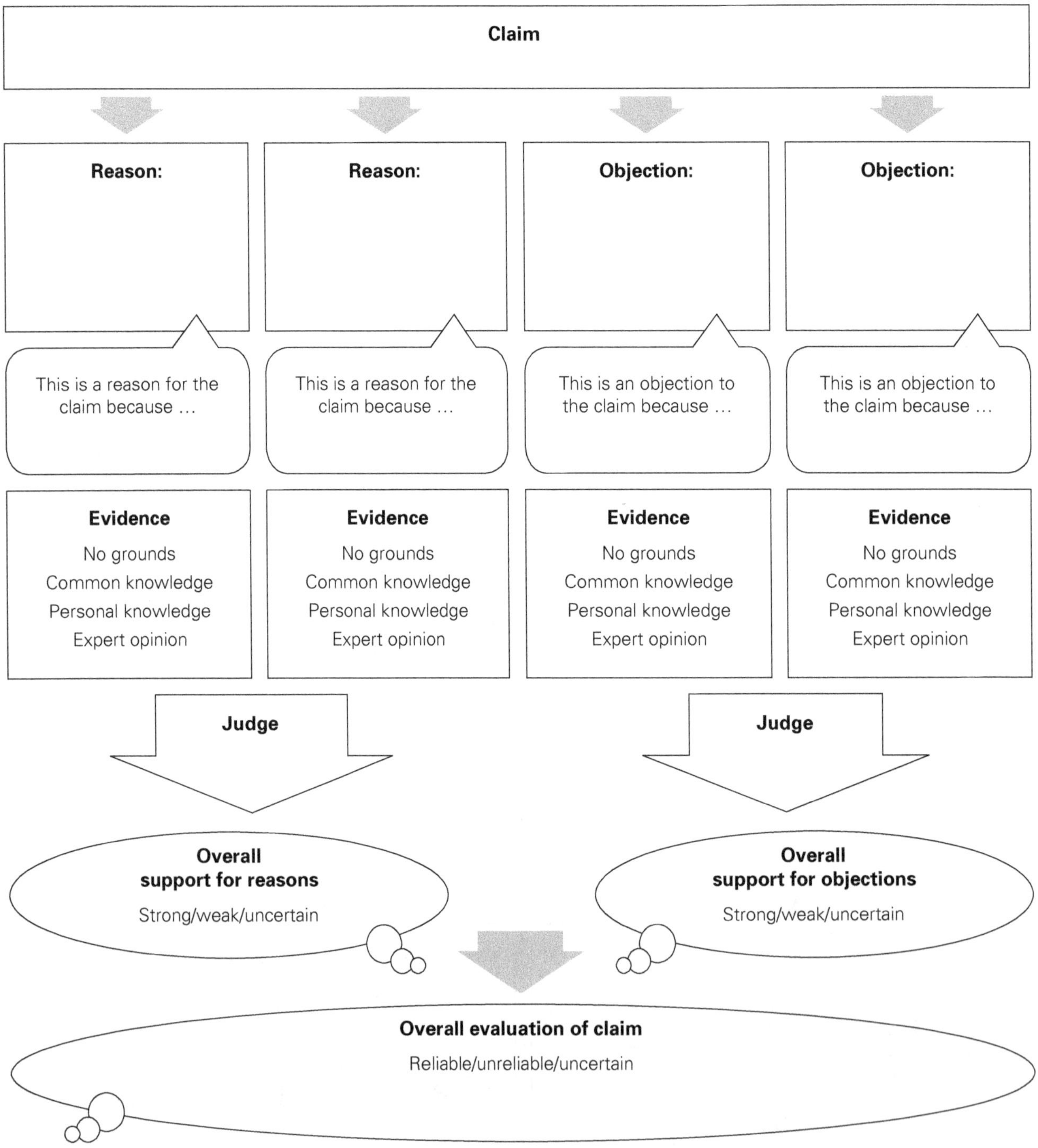

Claim

| Reason: | Reason: | Objection: | Objection: |

This is a reason for the claim because …
This is a reason for the claim because …
This is an objection to the claim because …
This is an objection to the claim because …

Evidence
- No grounds
- Common knowledge
- Personal knowledge
- Expert opinion

Evidence
- No grounds
- Common knowledge
- Personal knowledge
- Expert opinion

Evidence
- No grounds
- Common knowledge
- Personal knowledge
- Expert opinion

Evidence
- No grounds
- Common knowledge
- Personal knowledge
- Expert opinion

Judge → **Overall support for reasons** Strong/weak/uncertain

Judge → **Overall support for objections** Strong/weak/uncertain

Overall evaluation of claim
Reliable/unreliable/uncertain

© HookED, Pam Hook, 2015. All rights reserved. Adapted with permission from HOT SOLO Evaluate map ©Hooked-on-Thinking, 2004.

Exhibit 4.7: HOT SOLO Evaluate self-assessment rubric – declarative knowledge

Evaluate evidence	**Prestructural**	**Unistructural**	**Multistructural**	**Relational**	**Extended abstract**
Scientific argument	I need help to make a claim.	I can make a claim and give one relevant reason for and one relevant objection to the claim.	I can make a claim and give several relevant reasons for and several relevant objections to the claim …	… **and** I can explain why they are reasons for and objections to the claim …	… **and** I can give grounds for my reasons and objections (eg, variance, error, reliability, validity). I can judge their overall strength and thus the strength of my argument.
Effective strategies *(add teacher and student suggestions)*					

Exhibit 4.8: HOT SOLO Evaluate self-assessment rubric – functioning knowledge

Evaluate evidence	**Prestructural**	**Unistructural**	**Multistructural**	**Relational**	**Extended abstract**
Make claim, give reasons and objections, add a helping premise and grounds, judge overall strength	I need help to critique evidence.	I can critique evidence if I am directed.	I can critique evidence but I am not sure if my critique is reliable and valid.	I can critique evidence and explain why my critique is reliable and valid …	… **and** I can ask for and act on feedback on my critique of the evidence.
Effective strategies *(add teacher and student suggestions)*					

5. Interpret representations

Learners think about how data is presented and its effect on meaning – models, graphs, charts, diagrams, analogies and written texts. (Science capabilities, Ministry of Education nd)

Interpreting representations (extended abstract level)

Scientific data tell a story. Choosing different representations lets the data tell different stories. Being curious about the representations matters because representations can exaggerate or limit the story shared. Changing the representation so that it tells the best story is critical because each representation changes the way we understand the scientific phenomena. This capability encourages students to ask, "What does the representation help us interpret and what is hard to tell from this representation?" Interpreting representations is an extended abstract task.

Exhibit 5.1: Interpreting representations in summary

To **interpret representations** (an extended abstract task) is to ask: What is included and what is omitted from a representation? How is it similar to other representations? How is it dissimilar? What is privileged or exaggerated in it? What are its strengths and weaknesses? Who is advantaged and who is disadvantaged by it?	Example: Students create a representation of what happens when salt dissolves in a liquid, such as a 3D model using large marbles and particles of sand.

Exhibit 5.2 lists some specific questions students ask when looking at a model, graph, chart, diagram or written task.

Exhibit 5.2: "Interpret representation" questions for a model, graph, chart, diagram or written task

- How is this representation similar to or different from the other one?
- Can you represent this using a line diagram?
- What is easier to tell in the table?
- Are there any other ways of showing the data?
- Can you suggest improvements in this model?
- What is *not* shown in this model?
- Which representation better tells the story – the graph or the table?
- What do you think the graph is telling us?
- How can we best represent what we see happening?
- What are the advantages of using a line graph?
- What does the model misrepresent?
- What did the data look like before they were plotted on a graph?
- Can you evaluate the strengths and weaknesses in your model?
- What are the limitations in this representation?
- Can you create your own model for this?

Progress when thinking with the "interpret representations" capability

When we think with the capability "interpret representations", we ask:

- What do I know about interpreting representations? What is it? *Declarative knowledge*
- How well do I know how to interpret representations (directed, supported, independent use)? *Functioning knowledge – skill*
- How likely am I to interpret representations? *Attitude – will*
- How frequently (how often) do I interpret representations? *Behaviour*
- How flexibly (in different contexts, with different methods) do I interpret representations? *Behaviour*

Students can show progress in any or all of the above. They need to interpret (make meaning by classifying, comparing and contrasting, explaining etc) and construct representations of the science phenomena they observe or measure. They need to ask about the limitations and any improvements in existing models, and create and evaluate their own models of science phenomena. They use these various representations (models, graphs, charts, diagrams and written texts) to generate **explanations** and **predictions** about the phenomena.

It is important for students to realise that every representation is a simplified version of the real and, as such, every representation will exaggerate some aspects and gloss over others. Every representation will have advantages and limitations. Box 5.1 offers an overview of the opportunities and problems for some common forms of representation.

> **Box 5.1: Some opportunities and problems in using particular forms for representing data**
> - **Tables** make it harder to make comparisons or see trends.
> - **Pie charts** compare the parts in a whole, showing the whole and the parts in order from greatest to least. Pie charts are tricky to draw without a computer. They work best with a small number of parts.
> - **Bar graphs** are great for comparing facts or data of different groups and for directly representing data from a table. However, reading numbers in a bar chart can be hard. Changing the scale in a bar chart can misrepresent the importance of the differences.
> - **Line graphs** show change over time. They make it easier to see trends.
> - **Analogies** make links between the structure/function in an abstract scientific idea with that in a familiar real-life situation. However, they can introduce misconceptions.
> - **Diagrams** can be observational (describing what is seen) or explanatory (explaining how or why). They include titles and use scientific conventions for labels and arrows. They give a sense of scale and proportion but often omit data in favour of focus and clarity.
> - **Models (2D and 3D)** make a science observation or explanatory process visible by scaling it up. They make abstract ideas more concrete by simplifying the shapes that represent them. They can introduce misconceptions.
> - **Modelling** allows us to complete multiple trials quickly while defining known variables. It can limit the need to develop complex experiments and in some circumstances can be the precursor to experimenting.

Example: Using different representations to explain and extend understanding of chemical reactions

The rate of a reaction can be measured by the rate at which a reactant is used up, or the rate at which a product is formed:

reactant 1 + reactant 2 → product 1 + product 2

Some chemical reactions take place almost instantly (eg, mixing Alka-Seltzer tablets and water); others take a long time (eg, rusting iron nails or the weathering of rock). A curious mind would want to find out, "Why do reactions between common materials take place at different rates?"

Students can investigate factors that influence reaction rates using the reaction between Alka-Seltzer tablets and water. The moment the tablet is dropped into water, it starts dissolving. It reacts almost instantly, fizzing and releasing bubbles of gas into the water. The fizzing is caused by the carbon dioxide gas released during the reaction.

A simple investigation challenges students to explore the effect of temperature on the reaction. Can they make the tablets fizz faster or slower by changing the water temperature? How will they measure the rate of reaction? How much difference can temperature make to the rate of a chemical reaction?

How will they represent their results? How will these choices influence their understanding of what is going on? Below we look at three possible representations of the data: table, bar graph and line graph.

Using a **table** (Exhibit 5.3):

- **helps** by showing the three variables and the central tendency (the average) for each. It shows that the reaction rates were fairly consistent across the three trials, with the reaction rate in cold water being slower than that in warm and hot water
- **makes it harder** to see scale – the difference between each rise in temperature and the difference between each increase in reaction rate. A line graph would make scale more obvious.

Using a **bar graph** (Exhibit 5.4):

- **helps** by making it easier to see that hot water has a faster reaction rate than cold water
- **makes it harder** to tell the interval/scale between each water temperature – the scale on the x-axis is misleading. So it is hard to see any overall trend or pattern to establish a general rule. It may be better to represent the data on a line graph.

Using a **line graph** (Exhibit 5.5):

- **helps** by making it easier to see the trend of reaction rate falling as water temperature increases
- **makes it harder** to see the absolute value of the water temperature and reaction time.

The curious could affirm this effect of temperature by investigating other reactions where temperature plays a role in their everyday lives. For example, they might investigate the rate of reaction in light sticks in cold or hot water, or in bread dough rising in warm and cool environments.

Exhibit 5.3: Using a table to represent data on the effect of temperature on reaction time

Variable	Temperature (°C)	Reaction time (s): Time taken to dissolve tablet in water			
		Trial 1	Trial 2	Trial 3	Average
Hot water	82	21	24	20	22
Warm water	50	33	34	35	34
Cold water	8	141	140	143	141

Exhibit 5.4: Using a bar graph to represent data on the effect of temperature on reaction time

Exhibit 5.5: Using a line graph to represent data on the effect of temperature on reaction time

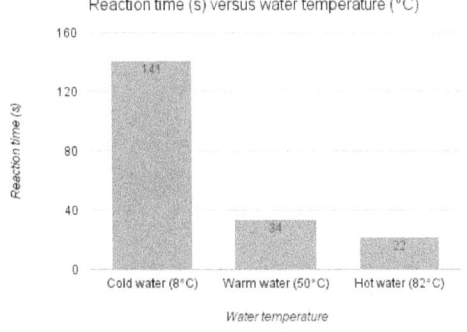
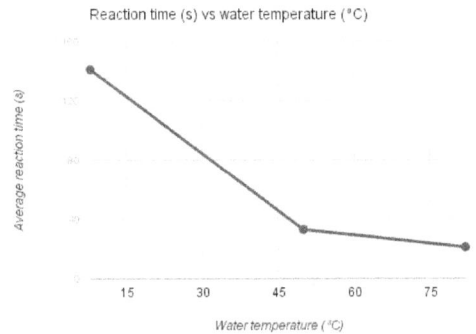

The influence of other factors. Other factors influence the rate of a chemical reaction, as in the experiment above. You might challenge students, "Can you come up with other factors that might change the rate of reaction? Can you design an experiment to test this factor?"

Students might then choose to investigate the effect of **surface area** on the chemical reaction between Alka-Seltzer tablets and water by chopping and grinding the tablets to increase the area available for reaction. The result will help them understand why some medicines are dispensed in powder form inside rapidly dissolving capsules while others are provided as tablets. The chemical reaction will occur more rapidly if the surface area for collision is increased.

When students start to research more about reaction rates, they will discover **collision theory** – the theory that the rate of a reaction depends on the frequency (or number in a given time) of "effective collisions" that take place between reacting particles (Box 5.2). So if they investigated changing the surface area of tablets available for reaction, they will have found that the rate changes as the surface area increases. Similarly they will find that the chemical reaction that results from burning wood in the presence of oxygen (air) occurs at different rates when they increase the surface area using a block of wood, wood shavings and fine sawdust left over from using a circular saw.

Note: Taking another angle on their experiment, students may realise that measuring the time the tablets take to totally dissolve in the water is difficult. When other students time the reaction, the evidence can become inconsistent – both less reliable and less valid. The curious will realise several ways to measure the rate of a reaction are available, including measuring the rate at which a reactant is used up or at which a product is formed. They can create other more reliable and valid measures to determine the rate of reaction, such as measuring the quantity of the reactant gas released.

Box 5.2: Collision theory

The collision theory is a model (or representation) that helps us interpret what we observe when reaction rates change. It explains that for a reaction to occur:

- particles must **collide** before a reaction can take place
- collisions must occur **with enough energy** for the reaction to occur (kinetic energy)
- reactants must possess a minimum amount of energy (activation energy)
- particles must approach each other in the **correct orientation**.

Thus the **rate of a chemical reaction** between two species depends on the **number of collisions** that take place between the particles in the different reacting species in a given time interval. Using this model, students can interpret that the faster reaction rates are caused by the greater rate of effective collisions.

Factors affecting the rate of a chemical reaction include:
1. increasing the **temperature**, which makes the particles move faster, making collisions more likely, and also increases the energy of the particles when they collide (activation energy)
2. increasing the **surface area** of the reactants in contact, which increases the likelihood of a collision and thus the frequency of particle collisions
3. increasing the **concentration** of reactants (or the pressure of a reacting gas), which increases the likelihood of a collision and thus the frequency of particle collisions
4. adding a **catalyst**, which increases the frequency of particle collisions (favourable orientation).

Not all collisions result in a reaction. Further investigation will reveal that an angle of collision (particle orientation) and a minimum velocity (activation energy) are also necessary. These ideas can be interpreted through analogy and a progress model, as shared below.

Analogy for activation energy and orientation

To score a goal, a player needs to give the ball the right amount of activation energy to get past the goalie and the ball has to travel in the right orientation to enter between the goal posts.

Using the analogy:
- **helps** us understand the activation energy and orientation required for a chemical reaction by comparing it with the energy needed to drive a football into the goal
- **makes it harder** in that it fails to convey how a series of collisions occurs between two particles. The chemical reaction is often the net result of many intermediate collisions, each of which may take place at different rates.

Process diagram

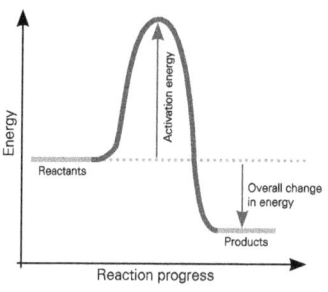

Using the process diagram:
- **helps** explain why most reactions we talk about do not take place spontaneously – they need a nudge to get going. The activation energy is needed to break the bonds in the molecules before they can react. It also explains why we might notice that heat energy or light energy is given off when bonds are made during a chemical reaction (exothermic reaction)
- **makes it harder** to see the role of orientation.

Strategies for interpreting representations

The following are some learning strategies (including SOLO maps and rubrics) to support students in interpreting representations of the material world and waste management.

Constructing a SOLO Interpret representations map

Exhibit 5.6 shows a SOLO Interpret representations map (strategies and prompts), based on the HookED SOLO Describe++ map, which is useful when students are learning how to interpret representations. They can also use the SOLO Interpret representation rubric (Exhibit 5.7) to self-assess this task.

Exhibit 5.6: SOLO Interpret representations map (based on HookED SOLO Describe++ map)

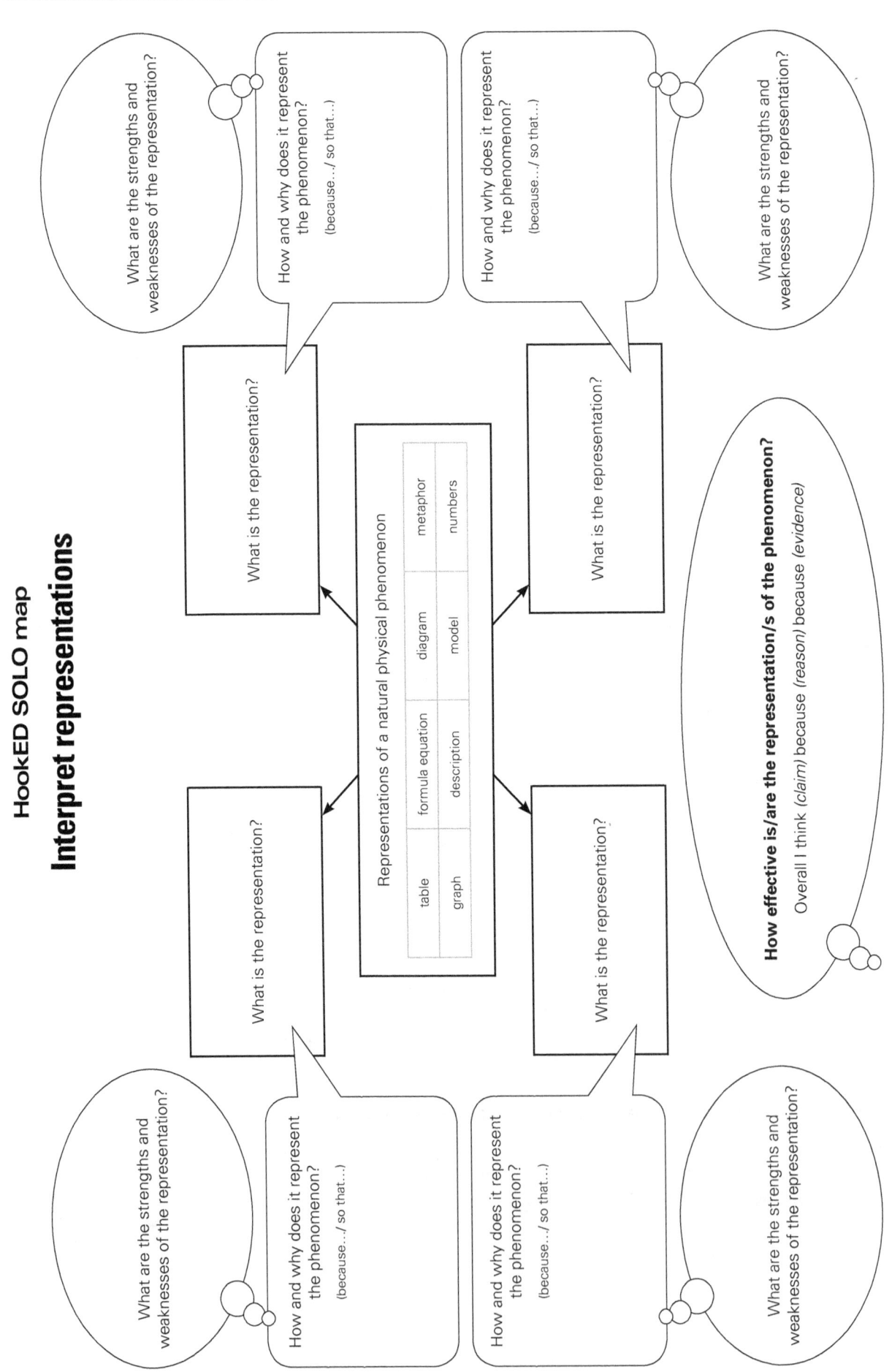

Exhibit 5.7: SOLO Interpret representations self-assessment rubric

	Prestructural	Unistructural	Multistructural	Relational	Extended abstract
Representation (table, chart, graph, model, diagram, analogy)	I need help to make a claim about what the [representation] shows.	I can identify one trend or pattern from the [representation].	I can identify several trends or patterns from the [representation].	I can support my claims with evidence from the [representation].	I can critique the [representation] and suggest an alternative.
Effective strategies *(add teacher and student suggestions)*					

Using SOLO self-assessment rubrics in constructing representations of scientific data

SOLO self-assessment rubrics can be used to support students in constructing effective representations of data they have observed or measured. The following examples focus on:

- constructing a table where students record their observations of some common materials (eg, carbon, calcium, magnesium, red phosphorus) based on properties such as: colour; solid, liquid or gas; brittle or bendy; dull or shiny; electricity conductor or non-conductor; floats or sinks; any other properties in common (Exhibit 5.8)
- constructing a line graph to show changes in weight over time of common materials (paper, food, metals, glass, plastics, other) found in school rubbish bins before and after a school-wide "naked lunch box" scheme starts (Exhibit 5.9).

Similar rubrics can be used for any other representation students are constructing.

Exhibit 5.8: SOLO self-assessment rubric for constructing a table to represent data

Functioning knowledge	Prestructural	Unistructural	Multistructural	Relational	Extended abstract
Title; Grid; Column headings for variable and unit of measurement; Far-left column for independent variable, class-sized intervals or categories; Missing values (–) and zero values (0); Cells for accurate record of numerical data	I need help to construct a data table.	I can construct a data table if I am directed.	I can construct a data table but I am not sure about it.	I can construct a table and explain why each feature is important.	I can make a claim based on the data in the table. I can compare and contrast the table with another representation in terms of how useful it is to represent data.
Effective strategies *(add teacher and student suggestions)*					

Exhibit 5.9: SOLO self-assessment rubric for constructing a line graph to represent data

	Prestructural	Unistructural	Multistructural	Relational	Extended abstract
Title – y-axis against x-axis variable for …; Independent variable – horizontal axis; Dependent variable – vertical axis; Scales – increase upwards and from left to right, divided evenly, adjusted to fit data range; Key if more than one graph on axes; Ruled lines if line of best fit is linear but not for smooth curve	I need help to construct a graph.	I can construct a graph if I am directed.	I can construct a graph but I am not sure about it.	I can construct a graph and explain why each feature is important.	I can make a claim based on the steepness of the graph line. I can compare and contrast the graph with another representation in terms of how useful it is to represent data.
Effective strategies *(add teacher and student suggestions)*					

Constructing a model to represent abstract scientific ideas in more accessible ways

Students might construct 2D or 3D models to represent an element made up of individual atoms, an element made up of molecules, a mixture, a compound, a metallic lattice and so on. They might construct replicas of previous models of atomic structure and show how those models have become more sophisticated as scientific understanding has changed over time.[4] Another approach is to role-play the particles in solids, liquids and gases as heat energy is added or removed.

Exhibit 5.10 is a SOLO rubric students can use to self-assess their work with models.

Exhibit 5.10: SOLO self-assessment rubric for constructing a model to represent scientific ideas

	Prestructural	Unistructural	Multistructural	Relational	Extended abstract
Constructing a model	I need help to construct a model to represent a scientific observation or measurement.	I can construct a model if I am directed.	I can construct a model but I am not sure about it.	I can construct a model and explain why each feature is important.	I can make a claim based on the model. I can compare and contrast the model with another representation in terms of how useful it is to represent data.
Effective strategies *(add teacher and student suggestions)*					

---

4 Go to The Science Teacher (http://thescienceteacher.co.uk) for resources on metallic bonding and atomic structure.

Using a Hooked SOLO Make an analogy map and rubric to construct an analogy or simile

The HookED SOLO Make an analogy map and rubric are used to find similarities between two objects that are normally not alike in structure. Using them to construct analogies or similes to represent the material world can help overcome student misconceptions about matter (Stavy 1991).

How do I use them? See Hook (2016), page 59.

Relevant tasks: Form an analogy: What is it like?

One example of an analogy for the emptiness of "matter" might be that the nucleus of an atom is like a housefly (nucleus) hovering in the centre of a rugby stadium (atom). When thinking about trees as carbon banks, sequestering carbon on land, students may make an analogy with sea mammals acting as carbon banks in marine environments.

Analogies can both help and hinder students' ability to think like a scientist. One suggestion for avoiding some misunderstanding is for teachers adopt a six-step approach (Harrison and Treagust 1994, cited in Boo and Aun 1997):

1. Introduce the target concept to be learnt.
2. Cue the students' memory of the analogue.
3. Identify the relevant features of the analogue.
4. Map out the similarities between the analogue and the target.
5. Indicate where the analogy breaks down.
6. Draw conclusions about the target concept.

Exhibit 5.11 shows how students used a HookED SOLO Make an analogy map to make analogies for mixing common materials. They were only able to come up with an analogy for mixtures where no reaction took place as the reactants would be able to be retrieved from the mixture.

Exhibit 5.11: HookED SOLO Make an analogy map for mixing common materials

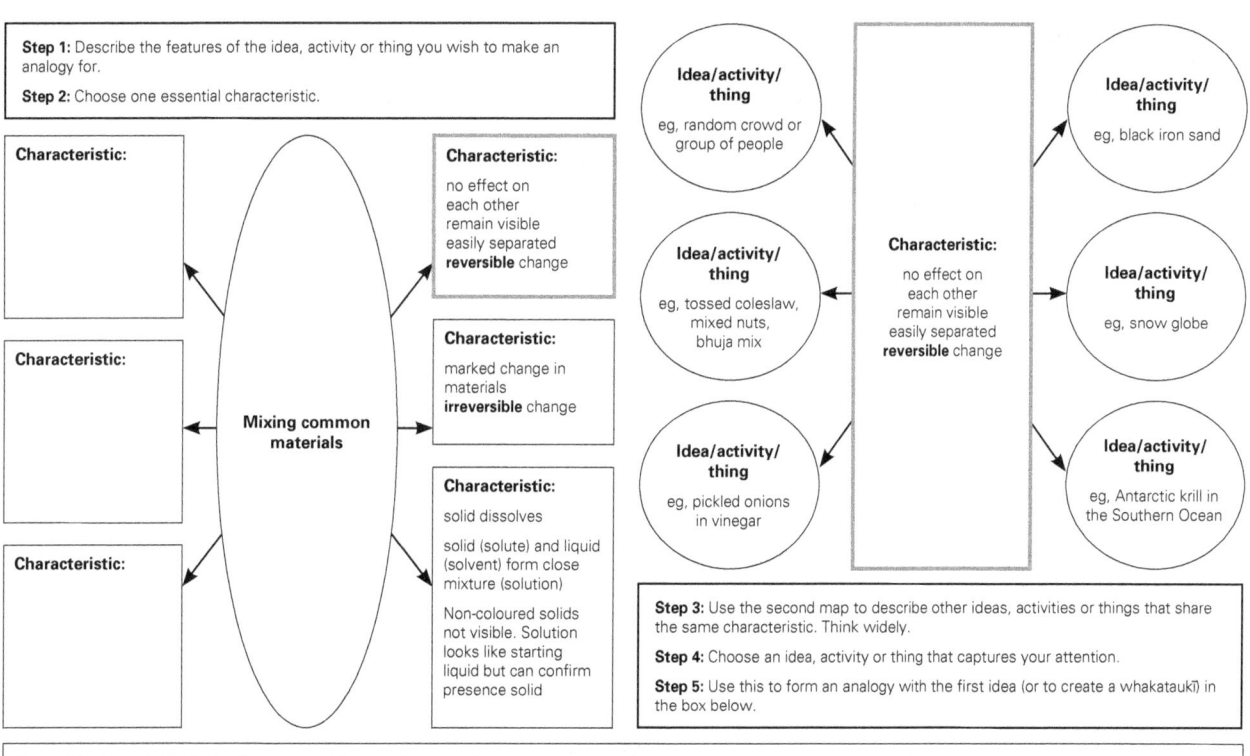

© HookED, Pam Hook, 2012. All rights reserved.

6. Sample SOLO planning and assessment

This section gives a range of ideas for planning for and assessing learning on the material world, using SOLO to make learning visible. It begins with an overview of constructive alignment as a way of aligning the central elements in this process: achievement objectives, learning intentions and success criteria.

Constructive alignment in planning and assessment

Teachers can use the process of constructive alignment and SOLO Taxonomy for any curriculum level. Here you unpack the achievement objective and differentiate it into learning intentions using SOLO verbs for bringing in information, connecting information and extending information (moving from surface to deep to conceptual understanding). In turn, the learning intentions are differentiated into success criteria (Exhibit 6.1).

Exhibit 6.1: Breaking down a curriculum achievement objective using SOLO Taxonomy

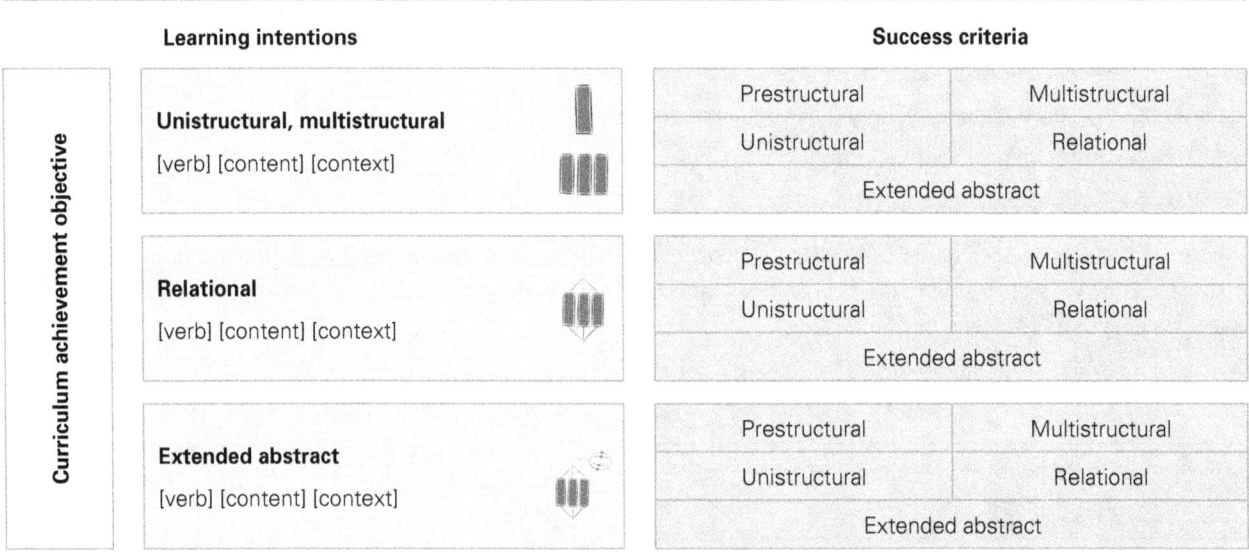

Exhibit 6.2 shows how this approach can be applied by unpacking Levels 1 and 5 science achievement objectives as learning intentions using SOLO verbs. You then choose from the differentiated learning intentions to plan learning experiences and to develop differentiated success criteria (see "Sample planning" on the next page).

Exhibit 6.2: Constructive alignment in NZC science – material world achievement objectives at Levels 1 and 5

NZC science – material world: Properties and changes of matter　　　　　　　　　　**Curriculum Level 1**

Observe, **describe** and **compare** physical and chemical properties of common materials and changes that occur when materials are mixed, heated, or cooled.

Possible learning intentions

[Possible common materials: wood, metal, plastic, rubber, glass, textiles]
Observe physical properties of common materials.
Observe chemical properties of common materials.
Describe physical properties of common materials. [multistructural]
Describe chemical properties of common materials. [multistructural]
Compare and contrast physical and chemical properties of common materials. [relational]

Observe the changes when common materials are mixed/heated/cooled.
Describe the changes when common materials are mixed/heated/cooled. [multistructural]
Compare and contrast the changes when common materials are mixed/heated/cooled. [relational]
Create an action to change a common material. [extended abstract]
Predict an action to change a common material. [extended abstract]
Plan an investigation to test your prediction. [extended abstract]
Undertake an investigation to test your prediction. [extended abstract]

continued ...

Exhibit 6.2: Constructive alignment in NZC science – material world achievement objectives at Levels 1 and 5 (continued)

NZC science – material world: Properties and changes of matter **Curriculum Level 5**

Investigate the chemical and physical properties of different groups of substances, for example acids and bases, fuels and metals.

Distinguish between pure substances and mixtures and between elements and compounds.

Possible learning intentions

[Possible substance groups: acids and bases, fuels and metals]
Observe the physical properties of a named group of substances.
Observe the chemical properties of a named group of substances.
Describe the physical properties of a named group of substances. [multistructural]
Describe the chemical properties of a named group of substances. [multistructural]
Compare and contrast the physical and chemical properties of a named group of substances. [relational]
Create a set of trading cards to describe common materials as superhero characters with their special chemical and physical properties. [extended abstract]
Define pure substance. [unistructural]
Define mixture. [unistructural]

Describe a pure substance. [unistructural]
Describe a mixture. [multistructural]
Compare and contrast a pure substance and a mixture. [relational]
Create a fridge magnet with a key to help others classify materials as pure substances or mixtures. [extended abstract]
Plan a process to separate any mixture. [extended abstract]
Investigate your process. [extended abstract]
Define element. [unistructural]
Define compound. [unistructural]
Describe an element. [multistructural]
Describe a compound. [multistructural]
Compare and contrast elements and compounds. [relational]
Create screenshots for an identification key app to help others distinguish between pure substances, mixtures, elements and compounds. [extended abstract]

Sample planning

The sample partial plan in Exhibit 6.3 demonstrates how declarative and functioning knowledge can be unpacked and developed within a unit of work. Each learning intention indicates the level of thinking needed. The success criteria allow the students to identify their current level of understanding and reflect on their learning at the conclusion of the lesson (to identify their progress and to feedforward their next step in learning).

Teachers can use SOLO verbs to identify appropriate visual maps to assist their students' learning. Activities around the science capabilities are developed within each learning outcome; having clear learning intentions and success criteria makes this easier to do.

Exhibit 6.3: Suggested partial plan for learning strategies and sequence of teaching

Learning intention	Success criteria	Lessons	Practicals and activities
1. To discuss the properties of solids, liquids and gases in everyday situations	M: I can *identify* solids, liquids and gases in a particle model. R: I can *explain* the properties of solids, liquids and gases using the particle model. EA: I can *apply* the properties of solids, liquids and gases to everyday uses.	2–3	Investigate blocked syringes half-full of sand (solid), water (liquid) and air (gas). Which ones can or can't you compress? Why? Investigate the nature of cornflour. Students visit 10 stations around the room and decide whether the substance at each station is solid, liquid or gas (eg, sand, water, ice). Students conduct role plays to show how particles behave in solid, liquid or gas.
2. To describe the changing state of matter using everyday examples	M: I can *define* the state changes of freezing, melting, boiling, condensing and sublimation. R: I can *give examples* of how common substances change states. EA: I can *predict* how a substance may change state if heated or cooled.	2	Heat stearic acid till it melts; plot the cooling of stearic acid or heat ice and plot the melting of ice. Make ice cream. Have dry-ice circus.

continued ...

Exhibit 6.3: Suggested partial plan for learning strategies and sequence of teaching (continued)

Learning intention	Success criteria	Lessons	Practicals and activities
3. To explain how particles dissolve in terms of solvent, solute and solution	M: I can *define* the terms dissolving, solvent and solute. R: I can *explain* the terms dissolving, diffusion, solvent and solute. EA: I can *discuss* how dissolving occurs in everyday situations.	2–3	Make a dilution series using potassium permanganate to explain concentration. Run traffic lights experiment (with different densities of sugar). Dissolve chocolate. Make crystals from super-saturated solutions (eg, copper sulphur, sugar candies or potassium sulphate).
4. To explain how particles diffuse	M: I can *observe* and *describe* how diffusion occurs. R: I can *explain* how diffusion occurs. EA: I can *identify* and *discuss* how diffusion occurs in everyday situations.	1	Investigate the effect of cold and hot water on permanganate crystals. Investigate the formation of lead iodide at the interface where lead nitrate and potassium iodide start to react.
5. To describe the structure of atoms in elements	M: I can *name* the particles that make up an atom. R: I can *identify* where these particles are found in an atom. EA: I can *predict* the structure of an atom given the atomic number and mass number.	3–4	How many times can students cut a 10 x 10 cm piece of aluminium foil in half? Cut 18 is about the size of an aluminium atom. In groups, students decide which of 10 samples of elements are metals and which are non-metals by testing their properties (eg, copper, sulphur, aluminium, carbon). Colour in the periodic table to show where metals and non-metals are. Carry out "pop" test for hydrogen gas and "glowing splint reignites" test for oxygen gas.
6. To discuss the properties of elements, mixtures and compounds	M: I can *define* the terms element, mixture and compound. R: I can *give examples* of types of elements, mixtures and compounds. EA: I can *discuss* the differences between elements, mixtures and compounds.	3–4	Melt jellybeans or wine gums (atoms) together over a Bunsen to make "molecules". Then put groups of the molecules together to show what a compound would look like "up close". Carry out experiments with separating mixture techniques: • evaporation – separating copper sulphate crystals from solution • chromatography – separating different pigments in inks, dyes or food colouring • distillation – using copper sulphate solution or coffee • separating a mixture of sand, sawdust, salt and iron filing.
7. To explain the information that can be interpreted from chemical formulae	M: I can *identify* the elements in a chemical formula. R: I can *count* how many of different types of atoms are in simple chemical formulae. EA: I can *interpret* the number of different types of atoms in chemical formulae involving brackets and coefficients.	1–2	Use play dough to create chemical compounds by having separate colours for different types of atoms.

Key: M = Multistructural; R = Relational; EA = Extended abstract

Sample assessment

The sample partial assessment shown in Exhibit 6.4 is a learning tool to develop students' declarative and functioning knowledge in the science capabilities. A major focus is on developing scientific literacy. Each section scaffolds students through the different levels of thinking in SOLO:

- Section 1 requires short, simple, declarative answers. Students tend to either know them or not.
- Section 2 develops students' ability to write their answers into flowing sentences and then into small paragraphs. It encourages them to link their ideas by using *because*.
- Section 3 involves one long answer. Students gain marks for completing the SOLO visual map (in planning their answer), linking their ideas in their answer and writing their answer well. When marks are allocated for aspects such as literacy and planning, evidence shows students are more likely to develop and use these skills.

Only a sample of questions in each section is provided.

Note that marks are linked to the SOLO thinking levels, to focus students on what they did well and, more importantly, how they can improve for next time rather than on what mark they were awarded. Presenting previous assessments to students before their next assessment improves their performance.

Exhibit 6.4: Matter matters assessment for learning – partial sample

Marking schedule

	Science knowledge score	Literacy score	Total score
Section 1: Think like a scientist	/20		/20
Section 2: Describe like a scientist	/12 (knowledge + *because* statements)	/8 (literacy marks)	/20
Section 3: Explain and discuss like a scientist	/4 (planning rubric mark)	/8 (written answer)	/12
Total score	/36	/16	/52

My SOLO level of thinking	Total score
Unistructural	Less than 30
Multistructural	30–40
Relational	40–48
Extended abstract	49+
My level of thinking is:	

Section 1: Think like a scientist

In this section you will be asked to recall facts you have learnt about this science topic. Good luck.

1. Decide if each statement below is true or false. Circle your decision.

    (a) Atoms come in different sizes and mass.   True / False
    (b) In gases, atoms are close together.   True / False
    (c) In solids, atoms vibrate in a fixed position.   True / False
    (d) In liquids, atoms are far apart.   True / False
    (e) Atoms can exist in different states, solid, liquid and gas.   True / False
    (f) Compounds are made of two or more different atoms joined together.   True / False

continued ...

Exhibit 6.4: Matter matters assessment for learning – partial sample (continued)

4. The following chart shows changes of state. Write the names of the missing changes in the empty boxes provided. Choose the words from the wordlist provided.

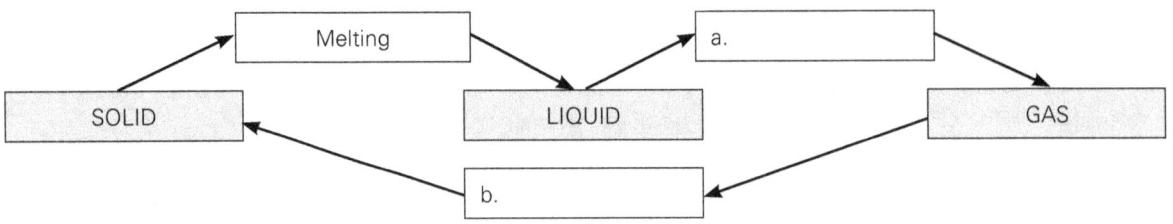

Wordlist: Sublimation, Freezing, Boiling, Evaporating

5. Solids, liquids and gases have different properties and different uses. Some are described in the table.

   Tick either one or two boxes in each row to show whether a solid, liquid or gas matches the description in that row.

Property or use	Solid	Liquid	Gas
a. It is used to build rigid or stiff structures			
b. It flows easily through a pipe or tube			
c. It can be squeezed into a much smaller volume			

Section 2: Describe like a scientist

In this section you will be writing topic sentences for each question. This means that you must "rephrase" the question into you answer. For example:

   Question: Name the three particles of an atom.
   Answer: The three particles of an atom are protons, electrons and neutrons.

   The question rephrased into the answer ↑   ↑ The answer to the question

2. The following list gives the names of seven substances.

   copper sulphate   gold   oxygen   iron   dihydrogen oxide   carbon monoxide   citric acid

   Name which of the above substances are elements.

   Science idea mark: _____ *Literacy mark:* _____

3. Copper sulphate has the chemical formula of **CuSO$_4$**.

   Write down how many atoms are present in the copper sulphate compound.

   Science idea mark: _____ *Literacy mark:* _____

   Because statements. For the next questions you must give a reason for either *how* or *why* something occurs. You must include *at least one because statement* to gain full marks.

6. When Hemi added some red food colouring to water, he noticed that quickly all the water turned red. This happens because of diffusion.

   Explain why the water turns red in relation to diffusion.

   Science idea mark: _____ *Literacy mark:* _____ *Because statement mark:* _____

7. Explain why an atom has an overall neutral charge.

   Science idea mark: _____ *Literacy mark:* _____ *Because statement mark:* _____

8. Explain why melting ice will change state from a solid to a liquid.

   Science idea mark: _____ *Literacy mark:* _____ *Because statement mark:* _____

continued ...

Exhibit 6.4: Matter matters assessment for learning – partial sample (continued)

Section 3: Explain and discuss like a scientist.

In this section you will be writing answers that require you to link your ideas and apply them. Marks will be given in three ways:

1. How well your planning page is completed
2. How well you answer the question
3. How well your answer is written

One experiment Hemi loved doing in year 9 science was set up in his class. Hemi described the reaction below:

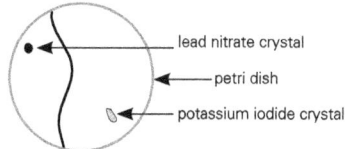

The two crystals were placed in a petri dish far away from each other. It appeared at the start that nothing was happening. After about 30 seconds a yellow solid appeared between the two. This yellow substance was a new product called lead iodide. This formed from the chemical reaction between potassium iodide and lead nitrate.

Explain the results of the experiment to Hemi in relation to solutions formation and diffusion.

In your answer include the following:

- How did the two crystals form a solution (include keywords dissolve, solvent, solute and solution)
- Define diffusion and explain how this process caused the delayed chemical reaction

Write your answer after completing the map (there are marks for completing this!).

Mind map – solutions and diffusion

- Use one set of **S**tatement **E**xplain e**X**ample boxes to explain how the two crystals formed a solution.
- Use another set to explain how the process of diffusion assisted the chemical reaction

S	
E	
X	

Planning map self-assessment rubric: Tick the correct level that you have completed the planning map to.

SOLO level	Criteria	Mark
	I can't complete any planning boxes.	0
	I can correctly complete one statement box correctly.	1
	I can correctly complete both statement boxes correctly.	2
	I can correctly complete both statement boxes correctly and I can correctly complete either one or both explain boxes correctly.	3
	I can complete the map.	4

Self-assessment

N0	N1	N2	A3	A4	M5	M6	E7	E8

Peer assessment

N0	N1	N2	A3	A4	M5	M6	E7	E8

Source of sample assessment: Adapted and abridged from Lincoln High School, Canterbury, New Zealand

7. Engage with science

This capability requires students to use the other capabilities to engage with science in "real life" contexts. (Science capabilities, Ministry of Education nd)

Engaging with science (extended abstract level)

The fifth science capability represents the integration of the other capabilities, enabling students to engage with science in everyday life. When you are curious and continue to develop and explore your scientific thinking, you can engage with science each and every day (Exhibit 7.1). This is a SOLO extended abstract task.

Exhibit 7.1: Different ways of engaging with science

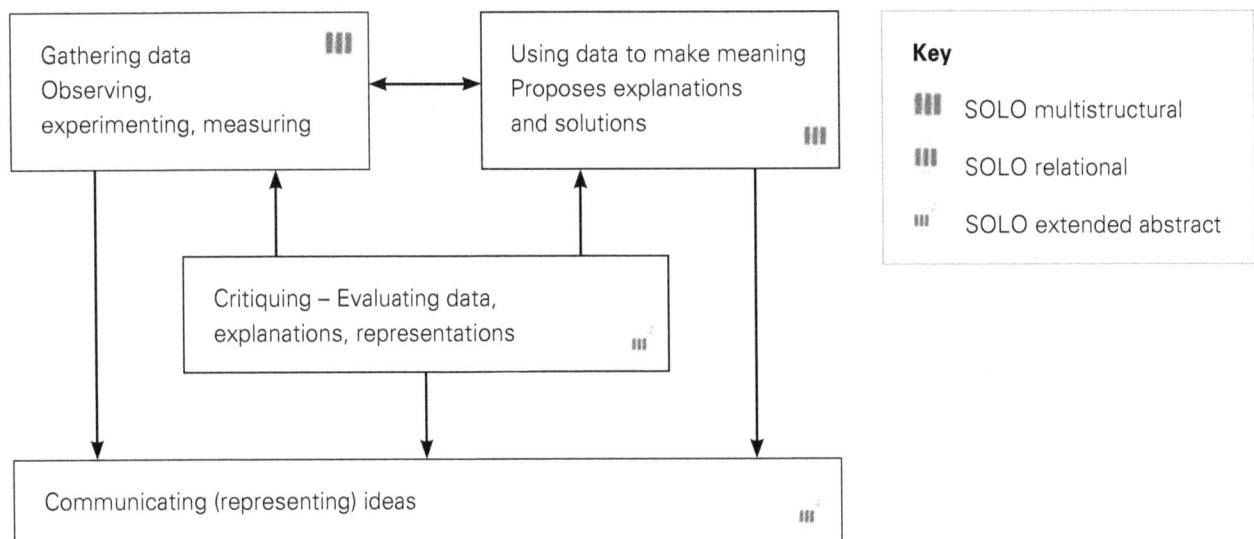

Progress when thinking with the "engage with science" capability

When we think with the capability "engage with science", we ask:

- What do I know about engaging with science? What is it? What is it like? *Declarative knowledge*
- How well do I know how to engage with science (directed, supported, independent use)? *Functioning knowledge – skill*
- How likely am I to engage with science? *Attitude – will*
- How frequently (how often) do I engage with science? *Behaviour*
- How flexibly (in different contexts, with different methods) do I engage with science? *Behaviour*

Students can show progress in any or all of the above.

Citizenship and waste management

Once students have moved from surface to deep understanding of the science of the material world, they are well placed to transfer this learning to acts of citizenship in an authentic material world context. Working with students to find the right material world context is nuanced work within and across school communities. The context must be a **wicked problem**: rich enough to provide multiple entry points and complex enough to offer no clear solution.

Dealing with our own waste or the waste of others (waste management) is a material world wicked problem. In a culture built on consumerism, where all activity is focused on selling goods and spending money (Exhibit 7.2), an immediate problem lies in how best to deal with the waste this activity generates. The context of waste management can be a local environment like a classroom, school or community, nationwide or global.

Exhibit 7.2: The culture of consumerism

- Work. Buy. Consume. Die.
- I want it, I need it, I buy it.
- Buy more stuff!
- Buy nothing day.
- I deserve this.
- Worldwide 99% of everything bought is no longer in use after six months.
- I shop therefore I am.
- More … I need more.
- We buy things we don't need, with money we don't have, to impress people we don't like.

Ethical consumerism explores ways to buy within (rather than beyond) your needs. It asks us to demonstrate citizenship in our dealings with the material world, in ways that benefit all people in all places and the planet.

With students' newly acquired deep understanding of the material world, we can design learning experiences to build citizenship for "democratic imagination, motivation and involvement" (Hayward 2012). For this task, Westheimer and Kahne (2004) offer a useful citizenship framework (Exhibit 7.3).

Exhibit 7.3: Citizenship framework

Personally responsible citizens:	**Participatory citizens:**	**Justice-oriented citizens:**
<ul><li>act responsibly</li><li>obey rules and laws</li><li>volunteer.</li></ul>	<ul><li>take a skilled and active role in groups that work for the common good</li><li>know effective strategies for collaborative action.</li></ul>	<ul><li>seek social justice, equity, human rights and moral rightness</li><li>take skilled action for social change</li><li>know effective strategies for changing existing practice.</li></ul>
Waste management examples	**Waste management examples**	**Waste management examples**
<ul><li>Uses recycling bins.</li><li>Brings a paperless lunch.</li><li>Reuses shopping bags.</li><li>Chooses not to buy products containing micro-plastic beads.</li><li>Walks or cycles.</li></ul>	<ul><li>Helps set up a waste food collection service for a social agency.</li><li>Is part of a street theatre group that demonstrates ways to reduce the use of common materials.</li><li>Works in a volunteer group to collect and recycle old cell phones, paint or cardboard packaging.</li></ul>	<ul><li>Explores economic, environmental and social sustainability in the context of waste management.</li><li>Takes action to address the culture of consumerism and waste management locally, nationally or globally, eg, by using geo-locating tags on local waste to increase awareness.</li></ul>

Source: Built from Westheimer and Kahne (2004)

These three levels of engagement in citizenship mean all students can engage with waste management. At each level they can:

- have a voice and feel they belong, matter and make a difference
- value, and act in ways that promote, community and participation for the common good
- experience agency
- demonstrate the rights and responsibilities they have as personally responsible, participatory or justice-oriented citizens
- make decisions and take action
- adopt a "sort it or report it" attitude.

The Participatory Science Platform (Ministry of Business, Innovation and Employment et al 2014) describes a remarkable opportunity for engaging with science (**www.curiousminds.nz/about/article/38/participatory-science-platform**). With resourcing and pilot programmes for students, scientists and community, schools have an exciting opportunity to collaborate on relevant science-based challenges.

As "The Story of Stuff" (storyofstuff.org) shows, waste management is relevant to a student's lived experience in and of the material world. Waste management is well suited for students to engage with science of the material world, with its multiple entry points and perspectives. For example, in engaging with the science behind reduce, reuse, recycle:

- personally responsible student citizens can study the decomposition of common materials through "rubbish gardens" and develop protocols and actions to address these at home or in the classroom, which they then follow
- participatory student citizens can study the access, manufacture, use and disposal of a common material like wood, plastic or metal and set up student groups to address these challenges in local communities
- justice-oriented student citizens can look behind the assumptions made in their school or community. For example, they might challenge notions of reuse in enviroschools that buy worm farms as a kitset rather than building them from found materials; or a school's commitment to water management when it buys coffee machines to train students for service roles in the coffee industry, which has an environmentally and ethically troubled water footprint (temp.waterfootprint.org).

Furthermore student citizens of all ages can think about waste management in many different guises. They can explore the challenges and opportunities for waste management of materials in their home, classroom, school, local community and/or nationally and globally as outlined in Exhibit 7.4. In addition, students can identify challenges at any stage of the waste management process, including during the collection process; how waste is treated; where waste is disposed of; and rules and regulations. As Exhibit 7.5 underlines, it is easy for virtually every student to find a personal, social or culturally responsive connection to the wicked problems of waste management.

Exhibit 7.4: SOLO framework for investigating waste management as a student citizen

Waste management	Highlight location: home, school, local community, national, global		
	Identify the issue	Explain how and why it is an issue	Wonder about possible solutions
Regulations for managing waste			
Waste treatment and disposal facilities			
Recovery and/or recycling initiatives			
Remediation of contaminated sites			

The following are some specific examples of how discussion about waste management can become an authentic and personal "wicked problem" for students.

1. **Lunch box waste:** The products commonly used to wrap food in lunch boxes are made from common materials such as wood, metal and plastic. Where do these products come from and where do they go after they leave lunch boxes? Why are they used? How does their use benefit and disadvantage people and the planet? What are their effects in the short, medium and long term? How were school lunches wrapped in the past? How are these products disposed of and what are the effects of this disposal method in the short, medium and long term? How should we address any waste management problem that results from wrapping school lunches?

2. **e-Waste:** The laptops, cell phones and other electronic products students use for learning are made from common materials like metals, plastic and glass. What properties make these materials useful? How are they are mined and manufactured? What is the real cost of mining and manufacture of electronic products in terms of depleting natural resources or minerals, air and water pollution, and greenhouse gas emissions? Find out about the complications of having the finite supply of these resources concentrated in countries such as China (for rare earth metals) and Bolivia and Chile (for lithium). What are the implications of having a short or highly controlled supply for current and future-focused technologies? As they investigate, students may learn that waste management of "discarded" cell phones is an issue and reflect on what they have done with their old phones.

3. **Hazardous waste:** Hazardous waste describes common materials with properties that make them a danger to living things and/or the environment – for example, because they are flammable, poisonous, strong oxidising agents, explosive, corrosive, infectious or toxic. Oil, paint, car batteries, mobile phones, swimming pool chemicals and solvents (chemical) waste are classified as hazardous waste. Students can conduct an audit of hazardous waste at home or school to explore how to reduce the amount created each year. What is hazardous waste and where does it come from? What alternative cleaning processes or recycling methods might be used?

Exhibit 7.5: Overview of many possible ways students can engage in the science of waste management

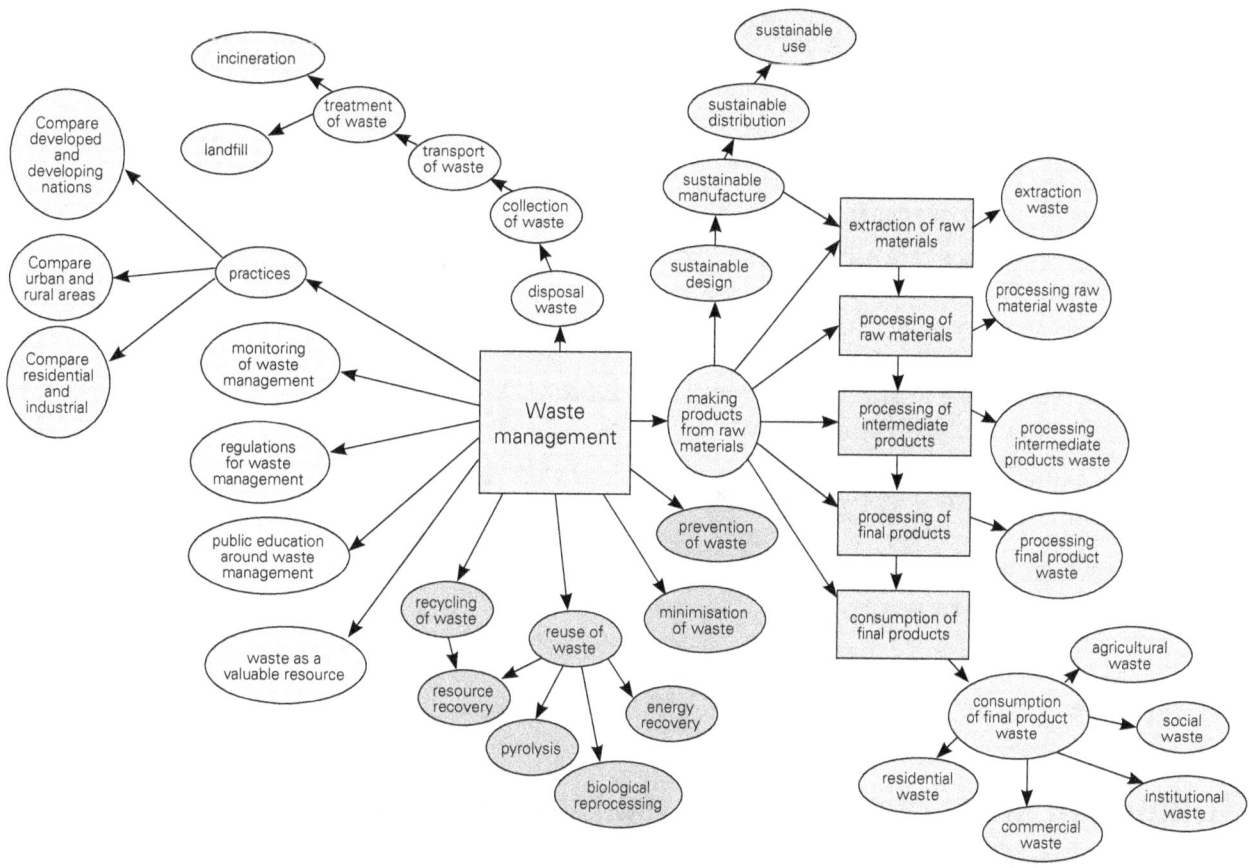

Box 7.1: Selected resources for students' investigations of waste management

The Story of Stuff: http://storyofstuff.org

Mental Floss. What school lunch looked like each decade for the past century:
http://mentalfloss.com/article/87238/what-school-lunch-looked-each-decade-past-century

Chris Baraniuk (2014) Stuff: Goodbye to the disposable age. *New Scientist*:
www.newscientist.com/article/mg22129621-000-stuff-goodbye-to-the-disposable-age

US Environmental Protection Agency. The secret life of a smart phone: www.epa.gov/recycle/secret-life-smart-phone

Todd Frankel (2016) The cobalt pipeline: Tracing the path from deadly hand-dug mines in Congo to consumers' phones and laptops. *Washington Post*:
www.washingtonpost.com/graphics/business/batteries/congo-cobalt-mining-for-lithium-ion-battery

Cisco Visual Networking Index Report: www.cisco.com/c/en/us/solutions/service-provider/visual-networking-index-vni

Nature Materials (March 2011), special issue on challenges of supply shortages of chemical elements:
www.nature.com/nmat/journal/v10/n3

Constructive alignment and engaging with waste management issues

When designing a plan of action for encouraging students to engage with the science of the waste management issue, we can use verbs at different SOLO levels to move students from engagement to surface to deep understanding (see Exhibit 1.1 in Section 1). Exhibit 7.6 takes this approach with learning intentions that use SOLO verbs to bring in ideas (surface understanding), connect ideas (deep understanding) and extend ideas (conceptual or transfer understanding) about the issue. Students and teachers can use them as generic prompts for learning about any issue about the waste management of common materials and to design their own research process into the waste management issue they choose to engage with.

Exhibit 7.6: Constructively aligned learning intentions for any issue about the waste management of common materials

Bringing in ideas (SOLO unistructural and multistructural tasks)
- *Identify* a waste management issue in your local community. [unistructural]
- *Define* the issue. (What is it?) [unistructural]
- *Describe* the issue. (What is it like?) [multistructural]
- *Identify* the raw materials involved in the issue. [unistructural]
- *Describe* the raw material/s involved in issue. (What are they like?) [multistructural]

Connecting ideas (SOLO relational tasks)
- *Classify* the waste management issue. (What group does it belong to?)
- *Sequence the steps* in the waste management process. (What is the order?)
- *Explain the effects* of the issue in the short, medium and long term. (What are the consequences?)
- *Explain how and why* there is a waste management issue. (What are the reasons/causes?)
- *Analyse* the issue. (What are the contributing factors and how do they work together to create it?)
- *Make an analogy* for the issue. (What is it like?)

Extending ideas (SOLO extended abstract tasks)
- *Make a generalisation* about the waste management issue.
- *Critique* (evaluate) the issue.
- *Create a new way* of addressing the issue.

These learning intentions are aligned with HOT and HookED SOLO maps and self-assessment rubrics to help students draft their ideas and monitor progress and next steps. In the rest of this section, we look at a range of these strategies.

Bringing in ideas about a waste management issue (multistructural level)

***Identify* and/or *define* task:** First, identify the waste management issue that most interests you by asking students to consult with peers: What is the waste management issue that matters most for young people in your local community?

Next, acquire and consolidate surface understanding about the issue, using verbs and learning strategies that will help with this task. For example, use:

- verbs for bringing in ideas – surface understanding: *identify, define, list* and *describe*
- strategies for acquiring surface understanding (Section 2)
- strategies for consolidating surface understanding (Section 2).

Describe task: What is this issue like?

The following is a sample task to bring in ideas about waste management practices in a local community:

> *Describe* the waste management problems and opportunities that a common material presents for young people in local communities wanting to use the resources from the material world in sustainable ways.

Use the HOT SOLO Describe map and rubric to support student thinking (see Section 2). Exhibit 7.7 is a SOLO Describe self-assessment rubric designed for this task.

Exhibit 7.7: HOT SOLO Describe self-assessment rubric for describing a waste management issue

Prestructural	Unistructural	Multistructural	Relational	Extended abstract
I need help to identify a waste management problem or opportunity for young people in local communities wanting to use material world resources in sustainable ways.	My description identifies one relevant waste management problem or opportunity.	My description identifies several relevant waste management problems and opportunities ...	... and explains why these waste management problems and opportunities cause issues for young people in local communities ...	... and makes a prediction about how young people in local communities might address these waste management problems and opportunities.

Connecting ideas about a waste management issue (relational level)

Interpretation is sometimes called the "holy grail" of critical thinking – the shift from surface to deep thinking. By explaining the meaning, students make a qualitative shift in understanding from surface to deep as they make links between ideas. SOLO relational verbs can prompt this thinking.

Acquire and consolidate deep understanding about this issue using verbs and learning strategies that will help with this task. For example, use:

- SOLO verbs for connecting ideas: *classify, sequence, compare and contrast, explain causes, explain effects, analyse* and *make analogies for*
- strategies for acquiring deep understanding (see Section 3)
- strategies for consolidating deep understanding (see Section 3).

Explain task: Why is this common material a waste management issue for young people?

The following is a sample task to connect ideas about waste management practices in a local community:

> **Explain** the waste management problems and opportunities that this common material presents for young people in local communities wanting to use the resources from the material world in sustainable ways.

Use the HookED SOLO Explain causes map and rubric to support student thinking (see Hook 2016, page 53). Exhibit 7.8 is a SOLO Explain causes self-assessment rubric designed for this task.

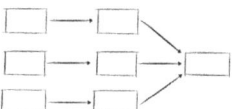

Exhibit 7.8: HookED SOLO Explain causes self-assessment rubric for explaining a waste management issue

Prestructural	Unistructural	Multistructural	Relational	Extended abstract
I need help to give reasons for the waste management problems and opportunities young people face in using common materials in local communities.	My explanation gives one relevant reason for the waste management problems and opportunities young people face.	My explanation gives several relevant reasons for the waste management problems and opportunities young people face ...	... and it explains why these reasons are relevant to young people ...	... and it makes a generalisation about how best to address these challenges with [local communities].

73

Extending ideas about a waste management issue (extended abstract level)

In this next step, we encourage students to transfer their new understanding about common materials and waste management to social, political, cultural or environmental settings; to think about waste management among developed and developing nations, urban and rural areas or residential and industrial zones in their local communities; and to look carefully at what they can do to make a difference in critical and creative ways.

Consolidate and extend (transfer) deep understanding about this issue using verbs and learning strategies that will help with this task. For example, use:

- SOLO verbs for consolidating and extending ideas: *generalise, predict, evaluate* and *create*
- strategies for consolidating deep understanding: seeking help from peers, classroom discussion and attempting to sort problems (Hattie and Donoghue 2016)
- strategies for transferring deep learning to new concepts: seeking patterns in new situations or finding similarities and differences (Hattie and Donoghue 2016).

The following are three sample tasks to extend ideas about waste management practices in local communities.

Reflect task: Overall what do you think would be the best solution?

Ask students to:

> **Draw conclusions** (generalise) about a "fuzzy solution" for the problems and opportunities that waste management presents for young people in local communities.

Use the HOT SOLO Generalise map and rubric to support student thinking (see Section 3). Exhibit 7.9 is a SOLO Generalise self-assessment rubric designed for this task.

Exhibit 7.9: HOT SOLO Generalise self-assessment rubric for making a claim (generalising) about a solution to a wicked problem in waste management

Prestructural	Unistructural	Multistructural	Relational	Extended abstract
I need help to make a claim about a fuzzy solution to problems and opportunities waste management presents for young people in local communities.	I can make a claim about a "fuzzy solution" …	… **and** I can elaborate on what I mean …	… **and** I can explain why it is a fuzzy solution …	… **and** I can seek and act on feedback from others to improve my "fuzzy solution".

Make decisions (predict) task: What to do next?

This is an extended abstract task and requires a different type of thinking. You can select the best possible solution to a waste management challenge using a decision-making grid as in Exhibit 7.10. The grid uses success criteria constructed by working with people in the home, at school, in the local community or in a national context.

Some examples of success criteria are suggested in the grid but the students and local community should identify the final criteria for a successful strategy. Note that the criteria should: be simple; address only one concern; use superlatives (*best, least, most, greatest*); indicate a desired direction; and be based on what you have identified as important for a solution.

Each group uses the established criteria to assess its strategies, giving each strategy a score out of three for each criterion. Students total the scores for each strategy and circle the "best strategy". They then explain why their group thinks it is the best strategy.

Exhibit 7.10: Decision-making grid to determine the best strategy for waste management action

Criteria for "doing something"	Score (from 1 worst to 3 best)		
	Strategy 1	Strategy 2	Strategy 3
Which solution will best manage waste from use of common materials?			
Which solution is easiest to accomplish with existing resources?			
Which solution is most likely to lead to sustainable outcomes?			
Which solution is likely to be most acceptable to the local community?			
Which solution will best help to reduce, reuse and recycle common materials?			
Total			

Get involved: Take action to sort or report a waste management issue for young people

Students imagine how they might work with other young people to sort out the waste management issue in their local community. What can individuals, classes, schools, clubs and youth organisations, local community, government and churches do? They:

- draft and then finalise a formal proposal and/or action plan to address the waste management issue
- research youth advocacy links that may help in taking the next steps and contact these agencies
- research their government representatives and learn how to take up their issue with them, if the students think that these representatives will be helpful in making progress.

We note that the type of action students take will be shaped by their age and the nature of the issue.

Student can self-assess their progress in taking action using a SOLO functioning knowledge rubric (Exhibit 7.11).

Exhibit 7.11: SOLO functioning knowledge self-assessment rubric for taking action on a waste management issue

	Prestructural	Unistructural	Multistructural	Relational	Extended abstract
Take action (work) to sort or report a waste management issue	I cannot take action.	I can take action if I am directed by someone else.	I can take independent action but I am uncertain about how and why I do this.	I can take collaborative action (work with others). I can justify how and why I do this ...	... **and** I can seek and act on feedback to make our actions more effective.

Conclusions

In the introduction we expressed the wish that young people might hold human endeavour in the sciences with a regard and curiosity similar to their view of human endeavour in the performing arts.

The budget available to encourage young people to be curious about and deeply understand the performing arts far exceeds that available for science and the material world. Young people are surrounded by data about the performance arts – they notice, observe, listen to, read about, experience and respond to the performing arts through popular media and discussion with their peers. They can make different links about different artists and different performances they observe (interpreting data) with their peers (chronological and cognitive). Finally they can engage in the performing arts at many different levels.

In this book we have used SOLO Taxonomy alongside the five science capabilities to help identify the knowledge, skills, attitudes and behaviours young people need if they are to be curious about and deeply understand science. In this way we hope to help students to become as curious and deeply knowledgeable about the material world as they are about the performing arts industry.

We have used SOLO to outline different frameworks and strategies using the science capabilities and to elaborate on ways to bring the excitement, curiosity and fun in the deep knowing of science to students. We have used SOLO to make the complexity of each science capability visible, and to develop success criteria to track progress in acquiring surface and deep expertise. This progress may be in gathering and interpreting data, using evidence, critiquing evidence and/or interpreting representations and then in identifying and taking up opportunities to use these in an authentic material world context like waste management.

Finally the book shows how science learning using SOLO and the capabilities demonstrates the futility of a simple demand for more "hands-on" experiences as a solution to "engaging" students with science in school. Without SOLO and the capabilities, hands-on activities too easily become science edutainment or busy work.

Many teachers already use SOLO and SOLO strategies (hexagons, mapping, planning and assessment) to good effect when teaching science, as the quotes below illustrate. We hope that this book will be a useful resource to strengthen their practice and to introduce other teachers to using SOLO as a model to develop students who are ready, willing and able to think like scientists.

> Comments from science teachers at Lincoln High School
>
> *As a beginning science teacher, I have found SOLO a really useful tool in making resources quickly and [it] allows students to understand the deeper concepts of the science capabilities.*
>
> *SOLO maps are great for scaffolding my students' explanations and build their skills for showing depth and comprehension within their answers. They allow the students to see a clear pathway to follow when answering sometimes murky NCEA [National Certificate of Educational Achievement] questions.*
>
> *I love using SOLO hexagons as they have so much scope for differentiation, so all my students can be challenged and experience success with them.*

References

ACARA. (2015). *Australian Curriculum.* Version 8.3. Sydney: Australian Curriculum, Assessment and Reporting Authority.

Biggs, J. (1999). *Teaching for Quality Learning at University.* Buckingham: Buckingham Open University Press.

Biggs, J and Collis, K. (1982). *Evaluating the Quality of Learning: The SOLO Taxonomy.* New York: Academic Press.

Biggs, J and Tang, C. (2007). *Teaching for Quality Learning at University. What the student does* (3rd ed). Berkshire: Society for Research into Higher Education & Open University Press.

Boo, H and Aun, T. (1997). Use of analogy in teaching the particulate theory of matter. *Teaching and Learning* 17(2): 79–85.

Bull, A. (2015). *Capabilities for Living and Lifelong Learning: What's science got to do with it?* Wellington: NZCER.

Chi, M. (2000). Self-explaining: The dual processes of generating inference and repairing mental models. In R. Glaser (ed), *Advances in Instructional Psychology. Vol 5: Educational design and cognitive science* (pp 161–238). Mahwah, NJ: Erlbaum.

Gabel, D, Samuel, K and Hunn, D. (1987). Understanding the particulate nature of matter. *Journal of Chemical Education* 64: 695–7.

Hans, V. (2007). *Judges, Juries and Scientific Evidence.* Cornell Law Faculty Publications. Paper 302.

Hattie, J. (2012). *Visible Learning for Teachers: Maximising impact on learning.* London: Routledge.

Hattie, J and Donoghue, G. (2016). Learning strategies: a synthesis and conceptual model. *npj Science of Learning art.* 16013.

Hayward, B. (2012). *Children, Citizenship and Environment. Nurturing a democratic imagination in a changing world.* New York: Routledge.

Hook, P. (2012). Teaching and learning: tales from the ampersand. In L Rowan and C Bigum (eds), *Transformative Approaches to New Technologies and Student Diversity in Futures Oriented Classrooms: Future Proofing Education.* Dordrecht: Springer.

Hook, P. (2016). *First Steps with SOLO Taxonomy. Applying the model in your classroom.* Invercargill: Essential Resources.

Hook, P and Mills, J. (2011). *SOLO Taxonomy: A guide for schools. Book 1: A common language of learning.* Invercargill: Essential Resources.

Kind, V. (2004). *Beyond Appearances: Students' misconceptions about basic chemical ideas.* London: Royal Society of Chemistry.

Ministry of Business, Innovation and Employment, Ministry of Education and Office of the Prime Minister's Chief Science Advisor. (2014). *A Nation of Curious Minds: He Whenua Hiriri I Te Mahara – A national strategic plan for science in society.* Wellington: New Zealand Government. URL: **www.mbie.govt.nz/info-services/science-innovation/curious-minds**

Ministry of Education. (2007). *New Zealand Curriculum.* Wellington: Ministry of Education.

Ministry of Education. (nd). Te Kete Ipurangi: Science Online – Science capabilities for citizenship. URL: **http://scienceonline.tki.org.nz/science-capabilities-for-citizenship**

Oshima, J, Oshima, R, Murayama, I et al. (2004). Design experiments in Japanese elementary science education with computer support for collaborative learning: hypothesis testing and collaborative construction. *International Journal of Science Education* 26(10): 1199–1221.

Rutledge, G. (2010). *Primary Science: Teaching the tricky bits.* Maidenhead: McGraw Hill.

Schrijver, K and Schrijver, I. (2015). *Living With the Stars: How the human body is connected to the life cycles of the earth, the planets, and the stars.* Oxford: Oxford University Press.

Smolleck, L and Hershberger, V. (2011). Playing with science: an investigation of young children's science conceptions and misconceptions. *Current Issues in Education* 14(1).

Stavy, R. (1988). Children's conception of gas. *International Journal of Science Education*, 10: 553–66.

Stavy, R. (1990a). Children's conceptions of changes in the state of matter: from liquid (or solid) to gas. *Journal of Research in Science Teaching* 27: 247–66.

Stavy, R. (1990b). Pupils' problems in understanding conservation of matter. *International Journal of Science Education* 12(5): 501–12.

Stavy, R. (1991). Using analogy to overcome misconceptions about conservation of matter. *Journal of Research in Science Teaching* 28: 305–13.

Stavy, R and Stachel, D. (1985). Children's ideas about solid and liquid. *European Journal of Science Education* 7: 407–421.

Westheimer, J and Kahne, J. (2004). What kind of citizen? The politics of educating for democracy. *American Educational Research Journal* 41(2): 237.

Index of exhibits

Applying SOLO to BIG ideas and understanding in the material world (Exhibit 1.6)	10–11
Big ideas about the material world as described in the New Zealand and Australian curriculums (Exhibit 1.4)	9
Breaking down a curriculum achievement objective using SOLO Taxonomy (Exhibit 6.1)	62
Building science vocabulary when using SOLO hexagons (Exhibit 2.13)	24
Citizenship framework (Exhibit 7.3)	69
Collaboration for dissent with SOLO levels differentiating task complexity (Exhibit 1.13)	16
Constructive alignment in NZC science – material world achievement objectives at Levels 1 and 5 (Exhibit 6.2)	62–63
Constructively aligned learning intentions for any issue about the waste management of common materials (Exhibit 7.6)	72
"Critique evidence" questions (Exhibit 4.1)	46
Critiquing evidence in summary (Exhibit 4.2)	46
The culture of consumerism (Exhibit 7.2)	69
Decision-making grid to determine the best strategy for waste management action (Exhibit 7.10)	75
Different ways of engaging with science (Exhibit 7.1)	68
Example of developmentally appropriate next steps, advancing by SOLO level +1 (Exhibit 1.14)	18
Examples of reversible and irreversible changes (Exhibit 2.21)	30
Examples of thinking strategies and e-learning strategies differentiated against SOLO levels (Exhibit 1.2)	6
A framework for classifying materials (Exhibit 2.26)	33
"Gather data" questions (Exhibit 2.2)	19
Gathering data in summary (Exhibit 2.3)	20
Highlighting a text to show the different SOLO levels (Exhibit 2.36)	39
HookED SOLO Describe++ map to describe, explain and wonder about changes when you mix two materials – vinegar and bicarbonate of soda (Exhibit 2.22)	30
HookED SOLO Describe++ map to prompt students to gather and interpret data and conceptualise the big picture (Exhibit 2.37)	40
HookED SOLO Describe++ triple strip map for BIG ideas in the material world (Exhibit 1.5)	9
HookED SOLO Describe++ triple strip map to describe, explain and wonder about changes when adding heat energy to or removing it from a solid, liquid and/or gas (Exhibit 2.23)	31
HookED SOLO Evaluate map for evaluating evidence (Exhibit 4.6)	52
HookED SOLO Explain causes self-assessment rubric for explaining a waste management issue (Exhibit 7.8)	73
HookED SOLO Make an analogy map for mixing common materials (Exhibit 5.11)	61
HookED SOLO Observe Infer Evaluate map for critiquing evidence for gas expansion in marshmallows (Exhibit 4.5)	51
HookED SOLO strip map (Exhibit 2.17)	27
HookED SOLO strip map to describe properties of carbon fibre reinforced polymers (Exhibit 2.18)	28
HookED SOLO strip map using three levels to describe a mobile phone's materials and their properties (Exhibit 2.19)	28
HOT SOLO Analyse map for a part–whole analysis of a Bunsen burner (Exhibit 2.31)	36
HOT SOLO Analyse self-assessment rubric (Exhibit 2.32)	36

HOT SOLO Classify map for grouping different kinds of matter (Exhibit 2.27)	34
HOT SOLO Classify self-assessment rubric for classifying common materials as solids, liquids or gases (Exhibit 2.28)	34
HOT SOLO Compare and Contrast map for two common materials – copper and sulphur (Exhibit 2.29)	35
HOT SOLO Compare and Contrast self-assessment rubric (Exhibit 2.30)	35
HOT SOLO Describe map with inference prompts to describe properties of metals (Exhibit 2.15)	26
HOT SOLO Describe map with prompts to describe the properties of a solid (Exhibit 2.14)	26
HOT SOLO Describe self-assessment rubric for describing a waste management issue (Exhibit 7.7)	73
HOT SOLO Describe self-assessment rubric for describing common materials (Exhibit 2.16)	27
HOT SOLO Evaluate self-assessment rubric – declarative knowledge (Exhibit 4.7)	53
HOT SOLO Evaluate self-assessment rubric – functioning knowledge (Exhibit 4.8)	53
HOT SOLO Generalise map for using evidence when gathering and interpreting data about gas (Exhibit 3.2)	43
HOT SOLO Generalise map for using evidence when gathering and interpreting data about the reactivity of metals (Exhibit 3.3)	43
HOT SOLO Generalise self-assessment rubric for explaining scientific phenomena using evidence (Exhibit 3.4)	44
HOT SOLO Generalise self-assessment rubric for making a claim (generalising) about a solution to a wicked problem in waste management (Exhibit 7.9)	74
HOT SOLO Predict map for using evidence to support and/or counter a prediction about factors affecting reaction rate (Exhibit 3.5)	44
HOT SOLO Predict self-assessment rubric for using evidence to support and/or counter a prediction (Exhibit 3.6)	45
HOT SOLO Sequence map for separating a mixture of salt, cork and sand (Exhibit 2.24)	32
HOT SOLO Sequence self-assessment rubric for separating a mixture of salt, cork and sand (Exhibit 2.25)	32
"Interpret data" questions (Exhibit 2.7)	21
"Interpret representation" questions for a model, graph, chart, diagram or written task (Exhibit 5.2)	54
Interpreting data in summary (Exhibit 2.8)	22
Interpreting representations in summary (Exhibit 5.1)	54
Making links using SOLO hexagons (Exhibit 1.11)	15
Matter matters assessment for learning – partial sample (Exhibit 6.4)	65–67
Mnemonic for the first 20 elements in the periodic table (Exhibit 2.35)	39
Mnemonic for the metal reactivity series (Exhibit 2.34)	38
Overview of many possible ways students can engage in the science of waste management (Exhibit 7.5)	71
Question prompts to consolidate deep understanding of solids, liquids and gases (Exhibit 2.33)	37
Questions to establish reliability and validity (Exhibit 4.3)	47
Sample of record sheet for observation and inference mystery bags (Exhibit 2.1)	19
Sample of useful scientific language for properties of materials (Exhibit 2.11)	23
SOLO entry–exit ticket – demonstrating the science capabilities (Exhibit 1.12)	15
SOLO framework for investigating waste management as a student citizen (Exhibit 7.4)	70
SOLO functioning knowledge self-assessment rubric for taking action on a waste management issue (Exhibit 7.11)	75
SOLO hexagons at the different SOLO levels (Exhibit 1.10)	15
SOLO Interpret representations map (Exhibit 5.6)	58

SOLO Interpret representations self-assessment rubric (Exhibit 5.7)	59
SOLO levels for demonstrating curiosity when exploring and participating (Exhibit 1.7)	12
SOLO levels shown through names, symbols, hand signs and academic verbs (Exhibit 1.1)	5
SOLO self-assessment rubric for constructing a line graph to represent data (Exhibit 5.9)	60
SOLO self-assessment rubric for constructing a model to represent scientific ideas (Exhibit 5.10)	60
SOLO self-assessment rubric for constructing a table to represent data (Exhibit 5.8)	59
SOLO self-assessment rubric for declarative knowledge about gathering reliable, accurate, valid data (Exhibit 2.5)	20
SOLO self-assessment rubric for declarative knowledge about interpreting data (Exhibit 2.10)	22
SOLO self-assessment rubric for evaluating secondary data as evidence (Exhibit 3.7)	45
SOLO self-assessment rubric for functioning knowledge about gathering reliable, accurate, valid data (Exhibit 2.4)	20
SOLO self-assessment rubric for functioning knowledge about interpreting data (Exhibit 2.9)	22
SOLO self-assessment rubric for gathering and interpreting data on a common materials walk (Exhibit 2.12)	24
SOLO self-assessment rubric for observing, inferring about and extending ideas about change (Exhibit 2.20)	29
SOLO self-assessment rubric for thinking like a scientist with the science capabilities (Exhibit 1.8)	13
SOLO self-assessment rubric for using reliable evidence to support a claim (Exhibit 4.4)	47
SOLO self-assessment rubric for using scientific language in relation to a scientific observation (Exhibit 2.6)	21
SOLO self-assessment rubric to describe, explain and extend a scientific phenomenon (Exhibit 2.38)	40
Suggested partial plan for learning strategies and sequence of teaching (Exhibit 6.3)	63–64
Suggestions for science attitude statements (Exhibit 1.9)	14
Using a bar graph to represent data on the effect of temperature on reaction time (Exhibit 5.4)	56
Using a line graph to represent data on the effect of temperature on reaction time (Exhibit 5.5)	56
Using a table to represent data on the effect of temperature on reaction time (Exhibit 5.3)	56
Using evidence in summary (Exhibit 3.1)	41
Using SOLO levels to differentiate science as human endeavour (Exhibit 1.3)	8

HOT SOLO Classify map for grouping different kinds of matter (Exhibit 2.27)	34
HOT SOLO Classify self-assessment rubric for classifying common materials as solids, liquids or gases (Exhibit 2.28)	34
HOT SOLO Compare and Contrast map for two common materials – copper and sulphur (Exhibit 2.29)	35
HOT SOLO Compare and Contrast self-assessment rubric (Exhibit 2.30)	35
HOT SOLO Describe map with inference prompts to describe properties of metals (Exhibit 2.15)	26
HOT SOLO Describe map with prompts to describe the properties of a solid (Exhibit 2.14)	26
HOT SOLO Describe self-assessment rubric for describing a waste management issue (Exhibit 7.7)	73
HOT SOLO Describe self-assessment rubric for describing common materials (Exhibit 2.16)	27
HOT SOLO Evaluate self-assessment rubric – declarative knowledge (Exhibit 4.7)	53
HOT SOLO Evaluate self-assessment rubric – functioning knowledge (Exhibit 4.8)	53
HOT SOLO Generalise map for using evidence when gathering and interpreting data about gas (Exhibit 3.2)	43
HOT SOLO Generalise map for using evidence when gathering and interpreting data about the reactivity of metals (Exhibit 3.3)	43
HOT SOLO Generalise self-assessment rubric for explaining scientific phenomena using evidence (Exhibit 3.4)	44
HOT SOLO Generalise self-assessment rubric for making a claim (generalising) about a solution to a wicked problem in waste management (Exhibit 7.9)	74
HOT SOLO Predict map for using evidence to support and/or counter a prediction about factors affecting reaction rate (Exhibit 3.5)	44
HOT SOLO Predict self-assessment rubric for using evidence to support and/or counter a prediction (Exhibit 3.6)	45
HOT SOLO Sequence map for separating a mixture of salt, cork and sand (Exhibit 2.24)	32
HOT SOLO Sequence self-assessment rubric for separating a mixture of salt, cork and sand (Exhibit 2.25)	32
"Interpret data" questions (Exhibit 2.7)	21
"Interpret representation" questions for a model, graph, chart, diagram or written task (Exhibit 5.2)	54
Interpreting data in summary (Exhibit 2.8)	22
Interpreting representations in summary (Exhibit 5.1)	54
Making links using SOLO hexagons (Exhibit 1.11)	15
Matter matters assessment for learning – partial sample (Exhibit 6.4)	65–67
Mnemonic for the first 20 elements in the periodic table (Exhibit 2.35)	39
Mnemonic for the metal reactivity series (Exhibit 2.34)	38
Overview of many possible ways students can engage in the science of waste management (Exhibit 7.5)	71
Question prompts to consolidate deep understanding of solids, liquids and gases (Exhibit 2.33)	37
Questions to establish reliability and validity (Exhibit 4.3)	47
Sample of record sheet for observation and inference mystery bags (Exhibit 2.1)	19
Sample of useful scientific language for properties of materials (Exhibit 2.11)	23
SOLO entry–exit ticket – demonstrating the science capabilities (Exhibit 1.12)	16
SOLO framework for investigating waste management as a student citizen (Exhibit 7.4)	70
SOLO functioning knowledge self-assessment rubric for taking action on a waste management issue (Exhibit 7.11)	75
SOLO hexagons at the different SOLO levels (Exhibit 1.10)	15
SOLO Interpret representations map (Exhibit 5.6)	58

SOLO Interpret representations self-assessment rubric (Exhibit 5.7)	59
SOLO levels for demonstrating curiosity when exploring and participating (Exhibit 1.7)	12
SOLO levels shown through names, symbols, hand signs and academic verbs (Exhibit 1.1)	5
SOLO self-assessment rubric for constructing a line graph to represent data (Exhibit 5.9)	60
SOLO self-assessment rubric for constructing a model to represent scientific ideas (Exhibit 5.10)	60
SOLO self-assessment rubric for constructing a table to represent data (Exhibit 5.8)	59
SOLO self-assessment rubric for declarative knowledge about gathering reliable, accurate, valid data (Exhibit 2.5)	20
SOLO self-assessment rubric for declarative knowledge about interpreting data (Exhibit 2.10)	22
SOLO self-assessment rubric for evaluating secondary data as evidence (Exhibit 3.7)	45
SOLO self-assessment rubric for functioning knowledge about gathering reliable, accurate, valid data (Exhibit 2.4)	20
SOLO self-assessment rubric for functioning knowledge about interpreting data (Exhibit 2.9)	22
SOLO self-assessment rubric for gathering and interpreting data on a common materials walk (Exhibit 2.12)	24
SOLO self-assessment rubric for observing, inferring about and extending ideas about change (Exhibit 2.20)	29
SOLO self-assessment rubric for thinking like a scientist with the science capabilities (Exhibit 1.8)	13
SOLO self-assessment rubric for using reliable evidence to support a claim (Exhibit 4.4)	47
SOLO self-assessment rubric for using scientific language in relation to a scientific observation (Exhibit 2.6)	21
SOLO self-assessment rubric to describe, explain and extend a scientific phenomenon (Exhibit 2.38)	40
Suggested partial plan for learning strategies and sequence of teaching (Exhibit 6.3)	63–64
Suggestions for science attitude statements (Exhibit 1.9)	14
Using a bar graph to represent data on the effect of temperature on reaction time (Exhibit 5.4)	56
Using a line graph to represent data on the effect of temperature on reaction time (Exhibit 5.5)	56
Using a table to represent data on the effect of temperature on reaction time (Exhibit 5.3)	56
Using evidence in summary (Exhibit 3.1)	41
Using SOLO levels to differentiate science as human endeavour (Exhibit 1.3)	8

www.ingramcontent.com/pod-product-compliance
Lightning Source LLC
Chambersburg PA
CBHW080046230426
43672CB00014B/2830